ENDORSEMENTS

I have had the pleasure of serving with Jeff at the International House of Prayer for the past ten years. I met him one day serving on a prophecy team that he happened to be a part of. His Scripture-based, encouraging prophetic words over people quickly caught my attention, and as each person began to weep as he began to prophecy over them, this quickly confirmed the accuracy of his words. His book, *Prophetic Like Jesus*, is simply an overflow of his life. This is what Jeff does and this is how he lives. He not only listens and prophesies the tender voice of the Lord, but Jeff is a wonderful teacher inviting others into the same close journey of prophecy, learning to hear the Lord's voice, and understanding dreams. I have watched Jeff walk this out for many years. In his book, Jeff writes, "He created us as spiritual beings with the ability to hear His voice and see with His eyes." Then he begins to unwrap the simple ways the Lord speaks to everyone. I loved this book and believe that as you read *Prophetic Like Jesus* you will also begin to see the simple ways the Lord speaks and the simplicity of taking His voice to every place you go.

JULIE MEYER
Worship leader, IHOPKC

Jeff Eggers has ministered prophetically to my family, and after tasting the fruit of his ministry I heartily commend this book. In these pages Jeff opens the book of his own life and lets you read the gleanings of many years. This guide to prophetic ministry will open your understanding and help to activate your ministry gift.

BOB SORGE
Author, bobsorge.com

This is the best practicable book on hearing God's voice I have ever read. *Prophetic Like Jesus* is a biblically sound resource for those desiring to grow in the prophetic.

Rick and Lori Taylor
Divisional Directors of North America
International Association of Healing Rooms

Jeff Eggers draws from many years of his personal experience in operating in prophetic ministry and in equipping the body of Christ, young and old, to prophesy.

Jeff's understanding of the absolute importance of knowing the Word of God and ministering encouragement, exhortation and edification to weak people with the tender compassion of Jesus makes this book a valuable teaching resource to grow and to equip others in the prophetic ministry.

ED HACKETT
Prophetic Leadership Team
IHOPKC

When I first met Jeff Eggers in 1971, I was drawn to his passion for God and the Word. We had both come from some similar backgrounds and had been swept up in the Jesus Movement that turned tens of thousands of young people into radical believers of Jesus Christ.

In his book, *Prophetic Like Jesus,* Jeff Eggers has given us a balanced, comprehensive, well-written, and easy to understand approach to a very deep subject. Jeff's years of experience in prophetic ministry make him uniquely qualified. Thankfully, he details for us just how easily God moved him into this powerful and fruitful ministry life. It becomes very clear that this ministry life is just as available to anyone who will venture into the waters.

Like a guide, Jeff leads the reader into the personal thrill of learning to be used by God. Nothing in life could be more exciting.

Whether you are a new believer or a seasoned saint, you will glean outstanding insights for your own spiritual ministry life as you journey through the pages of *Prophetic Like Jesus*.

DENNIS BURKE
Dennis Burke Ministries

I have known Jeff for many years and believe in him. His book, *Prophetic Like Jesus*, teaches us how to develop kingdom hearing in everyday life. Every reformer who follows Christ strongly desires to hear God's voice. Jesus told us that His sheep hear His voice, and Paul tells us that we all can prophesy and build up the body of Christ. People often disqualify themselves because they need equipping in a practical, natural and Spirit-led way for all the arenas of life. Jeff's book is a practical guide to open our hearts to the wondrous journey of prophetic ministry. Jeff lays out progressive instructions that lead reformers into kingdom hearing with hope. Jeff carries the Father's heart, and his book is a must-read for us to become prophetic servants and kings.

BOB HARTLEY
President and Founder of Deeper Waters Ministry
Kansas City, Missouri
Bobhartley.org

PROPHETIC

releasing God's heart to your world

LIKE JESUS

PROPHETIC

releasing God's heart to your world

LIKE JESUS

JEFF EGGERS

DESTINY IMAGE® PUBLISHERS, INC.

P.O. Box 310, Shippensburg, PA 17257-0310

"Promoting Inspired Lives."

This book and all other Destiny Image and Destiny Image Fiction books are available at Christian bookstores and distributors worldwide.

Cover design by Eileen Rockwell

For more information on foreign distributors, call 717-532-3040.

Reach us on the Internet: www.destinyimage.com.

ISBN 13 TP: 978-0-7684-0720-4

ISBN 13 eBook: 978-0-7684-0721-1

For Worldwide Distribution, Printed in the U.S.A.

1 2 3 4 5 6 7 8 / 19 18 17 16 15

DEDICATION

THIS BOOK IS DEDICATED TO MY WIFE, CINDI, WHO HAS BEEN MY partner in life and ministry for over 40 years. A more generous and caring person I have never known. Her patience, insight, and support for me as her husband in the ups and downs of our many years in life and ministry have been a constant source of strength, and I cannot imagine trying to do what I am called to do without her by my side.

I would also like to dedicate this book to the Prophetic Leadership Team at IHOP-KC, Ed Hackett and Graeme and Sabrina Walsh, for their many years of encouragement and insight into the gift of prophecy and prophetic ministry. It was a joy to work with you. Also, thanks goes out to my staff assistants, Brian, Amanda, Kelli, Liz, Tasha, and David, for your help in putting the foundational notes of this book to the test in all the internships you helped me teach and minister in. Bless you all. Lastly, a big thanks to Mike Bickle for providing such an awesome place for the seedbed of the prophetic to grow into maturity.

The phrase, "My servants the prophets," is used nineteen times in the Bible. God chose men and women whose hearts were knit to His heart to impart His word to. Those who would serve Jesus's Bride in the gift of prophecy must be servant-hearted in their administration of the gift. We are friends of the Bridegroom but also servants of the Bride.

CONTENTS

FOREWORD

JEFF EGGERS SERVED ON THE STAFF OF THE INTERNATIONAL House of Prayer of Kansas City for ten years. He served on the leadership team of our prophetic and healing ministries and also taught in our Bible school and internships as well as regularly ministering to many who visited the House of Prayer. He developed the content of this book in the trenches of day-to-day practical ministry. He addresses the basic principles of prophesying along with learning to hear and feel the Father's heart in the process. His ten years of experience in our prayer room as a worshiper and intercessor also come through in the encouraging and instructive treatment of the subject of cultivating a prophetic heart. The consistent practice of praying Scripture, gazing on the beauty of Jesus, and carrying the Father's heart for cities and nations is expressed as Jeff emphasizes the importance of encountering God's heart. This is foundational for walking in a mature prophetic ministry. The chapters on the Father's heart and the bridal paradigm invite those who prophesy to experience the wonder of a joyful God and the mystery of eternal partnership with Jesus in their journey of learning to serve the church with the gift of prophecy with humility.

Jeff's previous pastoral ministry and his traveling ministry and interaction with leaders have also contributed to his understanding of the integration of prophetic ministry into both the local church and the marketplace. You will find his practical experience in training and equipping to be helpful for you personally as well as for teaching and raising up those with prophetic gifts in your church or other arena of influence.

I believe this book will challenge, equip, and inspire you to not only prophesy, but to also see and love Jesus more, for Jesus's testimony is the spirit of prophesy (see Rev. 19:10).

MIKE BICKLE

Founder and Director of the International House of Prayer,

Kansas City, Missouri

PREFACE

AFTER SHARING THE SECRETS OF HIS HEART WITH A CO-WORKER, he was shocked. I prophetically spoke to him about his marriage and financial situation and what God had in store for him if he would respond. He asked me, "How did you know those things?" I simply explained to him that God loved him and gave me the revelation of his heart because He wanted to help him. He was in awe.

There is a real need today for the Church (that's you and me) to learn how to make God relevant to our world. Many believers long for a more vibrant relationship with God but feel stuck somewhere between what they know of God's promises and where those actual promises become reality. They are unaware that God longs for them not only to learn to hear Him, but to also encourage others through hearing and sharing Jesus's encouraging words to them. Taking this a step further, God also wants us to share His whispers, His thoughts with those who don't believe.

Most non-believers either consider the Church or religion to be a negative thing or irrelevant to their lives. Christians are often perceived as harsh and judgmental or as people who don't have a clue as to what happens in the "real world." We are marginalized, categorized, and very much ignored. The world doesn't understand or care about our doctrines. The world isn't looking for church or religion, but they are looking for life. The people you live with and work with and go to school with may have negative or inaccurate views about the Church, but they are still hungry for something that meets their needs and answers their deepest questions about life. They are looking for love that satisfies and power that brings change and hope.

What if you could be God's voice to that person who is hungry and searching? What if you could not only give them the reality of God's word, but could also reveal the presence of Jesus to them in a way that they know He is real? Paul said that the Kingdom of God is not a matter of words, but of power. I believe the Lord wants to raise up a people who not only know Jesus, but are also anointed to make Him known. We have been well fed for years, and now the Lord is challenging us to take what we know and release it into our world. It is a time for the gifts of the Spirit to move past the four walls of the Church and get into the marketplaces and homes and campuses of the unbelievers.

Part of that expression is the gift of prophecy. God wants us to learn to hear His voice so we can strengthen believers, but also so that we can make Christ real to those who don't know Him. When we share the secrets of another's heart through a prophetic word or a word of knowledge, it brings the God they think is distant or non-existent right into the middle of their lives. Jesus is suddenly relevant! When believers carry this life in them, people will come to church, and the Church will become relevant to a broken, dying world.

The Church should be the training ground where we learn to prophesy in a safe context, and where we can grow through the practice of the gift. But the Lord wants to speak to the broken and the lost as well. When we bring the reality of God's presence and gifts to the broken and hungry, Jesus suddenly becomes the most relevant person of the moment. Isaiah 61 becomes fulfilled in the divine exchange of the grace and love of the Father for the brokenness, pain, and emptiness of humankind.

The Spirit of the Lord God is upon Me,
Because the Lord has anointed Me
To preach good tidings to the poor;
He has sent Me to heal the brokenhearted,
To proclaim liberty to the captives,
And the opening of the prison to those who are bound;
To proclaim the acceptable year of the Lord,
And the day of vengeance of our God;
To comfort all who mourn,
To console those who mourn in Zion,
To give them beauty for ashes,
The oil of joy for mourning,
The garment of praise for the spirit of heaviness.
(Isaiah 61:1-3)

Introduction

GOD SPEAKS TODAY

GEOLOGY, BIOLOGY, OR PHILOSOPHY—I DON'T EXACTLY REMEMber what class it was. They all blended together on warm afternoons at the local junior college I was attending. All I know is I was bored stiff and a little sleepy, so when the class ended I was out the door.

I recall I made my way down the hall where a candy machine immediately caught my attention. There was a Snickers bar calling my name. I walked over to the machine and pulled out my change. But before I deposited my money, I heard a gentle yet firm whisper in my head. It was clear enough for me to understand every word, yet soft enough to be dismissed if I had not paused to listen. "You really don't need that candy bar," it said.

What? Really? Who is this? Could it be God? I asked myself. *No way,* immediately I rejected the possibility. Yet I was pretty sure it wasn't my own voice. After all, I am not one to talk myself out of a Snickers bar. Still, I couldn't deny it. The whisper was clear.

What would I do? That was the question. How would I respond?

THE WHISPER

I was born again during the Jesus Movement in 1970. I was one of thousands of anti-establishment, countercultural American youth who received salvation. And as a young believer, I became part of a church that was highly involved in the charismatic renewal of the time. Many charismatic leaders and speakers came to our church, teaching from the Bible and sharing their experiences. I was always hungry for more of Jesus and was intrigued by some of their stories, especially ones where they had heard God speak directly to them.

Additionally, I was amazed by the signs that they said had appeared to confirm their calls to missions and other evangelistic ministry. Many of these signs involved God miraculously speaking at just the right moment. I even heard one ex-gangster tell how God actually changed the radio station in his car so he could hear the gospel and get saved. All these stories, and the little bit of teaching I had on the gift of prophecy, made me curious about whether or not God would speak to me.

During that boring lecture I mentioned earlier, I had allowed my mind to wander. I thought of all the many stories and testimonies of God speaking to various people, and I decided to ask God to speak to me. I didn't ask Him to speak to me about anything specifically. I just wanted to hear His voice for myself. I remember thinking, *Would His voice be loud and thunderous? Would it be that mysterious "still, small voice" Elijah heard in the cave? Or would an angel show up with a message for me? Would I have a dream?*

I didn't know how it might come to me, but I was sure from all the preachers I had heard that, when it did, something dramatic would happen in my life. The heavens would open, people would get saved, and I would have a great story to tell. So you can understand my consternation and surprise when God simply said, "You don't need that candy bar."

So what did I do when He said that to me? I did what any hungry young man would do. I ignored the voice, inserted my change, and went for the candy bar! *After all,* I reasoned, *God doesn't care about candy bars! Anyway, He would want to bless me, not deprive me of the creamy chocolate, caramel, and peanuts hiding beneath the wrapper. He would only want to talk to me about the "big, important stuff" of life, not my diet.* With that, I promptly dismissed the voice and deposited my change into the machine, eagerly anticipating the liberation of my Snickers bar from its prison.

Nothing happened. It didn't drop. I put in my money, but alas, the candy bar wasn't liberated. I smiled and walked away from the machine. "Very funny, God," I said aloud. I guess He does care about candy bars!

This wasn't what I had expected when I asked Him to speak to me. No thunderous voice from heaven, "Thou shalt not eat that Snickers bar!" No whirlwind or earthquake. Only a simple voice in my head talking to me like a real person. I had asked Him to speak to me, and when He did I ignored Him. But that was probably the best seventy-five cents I ever lost.

In looking back on that experience, there are three things I noted:

- God does indeed speak, often in very simple, non-earthshaking ways.

- God wants to talk to me about everything, even the small stuff.

- And, finally, God is no respecter of persons. I wasn't a preacher or evangelist or church leader. I was a college student who also worked as a janitor for the local school district, and He still wanted to talk to me!

So began my journey into the prophetic. Since that initial experience, I have personally seen—and observed through many others—the power, mystery, and encouragement of both giving and receiving prophetic words. I have seen the Church be encouraged and edified by those who have learned that God still speaks today. And why should that surprise us? He is, by His very nature, a revelatory God who knows and uses many languages and expressions that communicate His heart and Being. Many Bible writers attest to this.

King David expounded on creation's 24/7 worship service in Psalm 19:1-4, where:

> *The heavens declare the glory of God; and the firmament shows His handiwork. Day unto day utters speech, and night unto night reveals knowledge. There is no speech nor language where their voice is not heard. Their line has gone out through all the earth, and their words to the end of the world.*

God also spoke to the prophets through phrases, visions, impressions, dreams, words, and encounters.

Through the prophet Joel, for example, God promised that a time would come when He would pour out His Spirit on all flesh. One of the signs of this would be that sons and daughters would prophesy, old men would dream dreams, and young men would have visions (see Joel 2:28). The author of Hebrews tells us in chapter one that, in these last days, God has chosen to speak to us through His Son, Jesus. Revelation 19:10 tells us that His testimony is the Spirit of prophecy. The apostle Paul tells us in Colossians 1 that Jesus is the image of the invisible God, that all things have their being and are sustained by Him, and that all of life will find its culmination in Him. He is the head over the Church and God's final word in terms of divine revelation to humankind. There will be no more messiahs, nor will there be any more inspired revelation that is equal to our Scriptures.

As Head over His Bride, Jesus still speaks to her through His Word. He promised the disciples that He would send them the Holy Spirit to live in them and teach them His ways. On the Day of Pentecost, the Father sent the promised Holy Spirit on a little fledgling prayer meeting in an upper room. Wind, fire, and tongues broke out as the disciples were overcome with the presence of the Holy Spirit in that room. In scene two, they were all in the street (with no explanation of how they got there), and many accused them of being drunk because of their odd speech and behavior. Peter stood up and preached, explaining that this was the fulfillment of Joel 2:28. From that point on, the Holy Spirit became available to dwell in all who called on the name of the Lord, not just a few select prophets.

According to the apostle Paul, when Jesus rose from the grave, He carried "captivity captive, and gave gifts to men" (Eph. 4:8). The Holy Spirit became the administrator of the gifts that Jesus gave to the Church, and one of the best gifts is prophecy, which brings me back to the title of this chapter.

Throughout the Word of God, we have evidence and support that He desires to speak to and through His people. The gift of prophecy mentioned in First Corinthians 12 is one of those ways.

THE GIFT

I remember a story about my friend who was ministering out of state. She stayed at the home of a woman who was a member of the church she was visiting. One evening, the woman listened to a tape of a prophetic word she had received at International House of Prayer-Kansas City (IHOP-KC) prophecy rooms. My friend recognized the voice on the tape, which happened to be mine, and mentioned to the lady that she knew me. The woman told her the word she received had been such strength to her in the season she was in that she listened to it often.

It is the kiss of God to encourage the hearts of His children through prophetic words. He wants us to know Him, hear His voice, and speak His words of strength and encouragement to His Bride.

I have been involved with hands-on teaching and training in prophetic ministry in one way or another for more than twenty-five years. It has been my joy to watch people's hearts come alive with the wonder and excitement of hearing God's voice for themselves. Furthermore, I have witnessed these people then speak prophetic words to others that encourage and strengthen them in practical ways in their journey. Many have found this simple place of prophetic ministry to be such an encouraging way to serve the Church. Such observations and experiences in my own journey are what led me to the write this book. The same simple points that God taught me from the beginning are still true.

- He speaks to people, most often in non-earthshattering ways, but significant ways nonetheless.

- He is interested in talking to people about all the aspects of their lives, great and small.

- And He is no respecter of persons.

Yes, God speaks, as Joel stated, to the young and the old, to men and women in all states of life—educated or not, in the home, in the church, on the streets, or in the marketplace. I believe God wants you to know that He wants to speak to and through you! He wants to use you to "wash the feet of the saints" with timely words of encouragement.

THE GOAL

Understanding that God has given prophecy as a gift to build up His Church, my personal goal, then, is to equip you to prophesy—not once or twice, but rather throughout your journey—from a heart that grows deep in God and impacts folks over a lifetime of service. My emphasis will be on personal prophecy, though corporate prophecy may be addressed on occasion.

You can find more scholarly works in defense and explanation of the gift of prophecy for today, and you can find books that will give you a more comprehensive view of prophets and the prophetic movement. I love books like these, and I find them very helpful as a student of the prophetic. But my purpose was to write a book that encourages each and every believer to allow himself or herself to be used of God in prophecy.

If your desire is to understand, grow, and serve the body in prophesying and prophetic ministry, I think you will be blessed, challenged, and encouraged by what you find in the pages that follow. I generally take a "blue collar" approach to equipping, meaning that I take a direct, "roll up my sleeves and jump in" approach. So, together, we will jump head on into the main principles relating to personal prophecy, to both understand and practice them.

Whether you are new to the subject or have some experience in prophetic ministry, I believe this book will help you move forward in the development of the gift of prophecy. Whatever your religious background or denominational affiliation is, you can receive and minister in the gift of prophecy. I have done conferences and seminars with Roman Catholics, Protestants of different denominations, marketplace people, and church people and can say with some boldness that God really is no respecter of persons. We bring our open, hungry hearts, and God responds with mercy, grace, and gifts of the Holy Spirit.

To achieve my goal for this book, I want to build on four key areas:

- God wants the entire Church to hear His voice and move in the gifts and callings He has placed within her.

- We all have a desire to be significant and make an impact in the earth, and the gift of prophecy is one way to walk out that desire.

- We need to develop a lifestyle that supports and yet goes beyond the gift of prophecy.

- Leaders need to equip the saints to minister in the prophetic.

THE PARADIGM

I desire for people to learn to hear and speak God's heart in a variety of arenas. Everyone gets to play in the Kingdom. God would that we all prophesy, so there are no lone superstars.

I want to break the paradigm that some have about *platform prophecy* being the norm as the main expression of prophetic ministry. I am not against platform prophecy (the practice of prophesying over people from the stage or platform in church- or conference-type settings). At times, I do this myself. But that is not the main arena that most people will prophesy in, nor does that expression of the prophetic make it any more powerful than it can be in the marketplace or on the school campus. If you have seen the prophetic expressed in that way and said, "I can't relate to that," or "I could never do that," don't worry. You don't have to. The late John Wimber coined the phrase, "naturally supernatural," meaning that God wants to release the gifts of the Spirit in simple, natural ways in both church and non-church settings.

Each of us desires to be or do something significant. We want to impact the lives of others. I have met so many believers whose whole concept of ministry is defined by what takes place within the four walls of their church. They want to have impact, but they aren't preachers or singers or Sunday school teachers. Though they may be encouraged in church by the sermon, worship, or fellow believers, they don't see a place for the expression of their gifts or callings. This lack of expression stunts their potential and, in many cases, causes them to draw back from any type of practical ministry.

God created all of us for greatness and to impact the arenas of life He has placed us in. Learning to function and grow in the realm of the prophetic is one avenue where believers can find an expression of significance and impact within and without the four walls of their church.

While the process of functioning in the gift of prophecy can be exhilarating, exciting, and fulfilling, in itself it can't satisfy our deepest spiritual desires. The gift flows best from a heart that is growing deep in the garden of God's heart.

Finally, the Church is in need of leaders to equip the saints to minister in the prophetic. These need to be ready to address the challenges of prophetic ministry in churches and small groups.

THE APPROACH

So the journey begins! You will find this book is laid out in progressive sections. Section One is *The Quick Start Guide*. I have noticed that when I buy any new electronic item, there is usually a detailed owner's manual and a *quick start* guide. The quick start guide is designed to help you begin using the product immediately, while the detailed manual is to help you understand more intricate features of the device.

Section One is designed to equip you to prophesy starting today! The good thing about this quick start guide is that the basic principles that get you started also lay a foundation for going deeper and becoming more skillful in the gift as you continue to practice it.

The second section provides a context for growing deep into God's heart. When we prophesy, we are representing the communication of God's heart to another person. Therefore, we want our perceptions of Him to be correct, and we want to learn to see how He sees and feel how He feels. As one of my prophetic friends has told me on a couple of occasions, "The Father is looking for friends to share His secrets with, not information brokers who are trying to establish prophetic platforms." In this section, the emphasis will be on understanding the Father's heart, who we are as the Bride, and how to deepen our intimacy with Him.

The thrust of Section Three goes to the heart of learning to prophesy from the perspective of a servant. Functioning in the gift of prophecy is very rewarding and can bring great joy, but at the end of the day, the gift isn't for me, it's for the body of Christ, and I must learn to release the gift as a servant to His Bride.

The last section gives practical instructions for leaders in both opening the door to the prophetic in their respective arenas and in training others to develop their gifts and prophesy.

On a final note, each chapter ends with a subsection titled, "Getting Plugged In." These simple questions and exercises will provoke your thinking and strengthen your prophetic gift.

Without any further ado, let's roll up our sleeves and get going with our *The Quick Start Guide!*

THE QUICK START GUIDE

My journey into the gift of prophecy and prophetic ministry has had many twists and turns. It has paralleled my journey into the heart of the Father in that, like my fellowship with Abba, prophetic ministry has deepened and become more personal through the years.

Two things about the prophetic continue to stand out to me. First is the simplicity of prophesying. Abba speaks to His children, and He delights in having them share His words with others. In terms of the act of prophesying, it is the result of simple family communication. Abba tells one child to go and bless another child by speaking words of specific affirmation and encouragement. The messenger can be a brand-new child who has just been born into the family, or an older mature child who has many more years of practice in understanding not only his Father's voice, but also his Father's heart. Either way, the gift of prophecy is simply received by sons and daughters who ask, listen, wait, hear, and respond.

The point of the quick start guide is to help define that process and make prophesying the joyful, simple task I believe it was meant to be. Quick start guides generally help you understand and enjoy a product sooner, leaving the more intricate details about that product in a lengthier owner's manual. So here, my hope is that you will gain the confidence in this section to begin your journey into the gift of prophecy which flows out of the Father's heart.

The second thing about the prophetic that continues to stand out to me is the *mystery* side of the prophetic. Though it is often simple, it always carries an *air* of wonder. I think it is important to understand this side so that the prophetic and prophesying never become casual or mundane to us, and also so that we don't confuse the simplicity of prophesying with the depth and wonder of the prophetic words we release.

The mystery lies in the depths of what the Father knows about the heart of one of His children. He gives another one of His children what seems to be such a simple message. That child only touches the tip of the iceberg in his understanding of what the word is designed to do and the power it will carry to the heart of the receiver. He simply repeats a phrase, relays an impression, shares a picture—things that to him are simple, unconnected puzzle pieces. But to the target they are aimed at, they are words of life. They supply a stake in the ground of hope. They tell another child that his Father hears and sees and knows where he is, that He is attentive to his prayers and has come alongside. Therein lies the mystery and the simplicity of the gift of prophecy. I never cease to be amazed at how words and impressions that seem so simple to me can completely undo the heart of another when he or she receives them.

The good thing about this quick start guide is that it also contains within it the foundations of the owner's manual. The basic principles of the operation of the gift don't change. It is not the understanding of the gift and the reception of divine information that leads to a deeper knowledge of moving in the prophetic. It is the deeper heart connection to the Father's heart that takes the gift into maturity and greater anointing. To demonstrate this, I go back to my earlier analogy of a new child and a more mature child. The new child is excited about hearing his Father's voice, but he hasn't yet learned the nuances of the Father's heart. The more mature child, through practice, has gained a deeper understanding of the heart behind the voice. The principles remain constant, but the depth of fellowship and intimacy know no ceiling. So this quick start guide provides the opportunity for both the basic training and the advanced heart lessons. May you enjoy your simple and mysterious journey into growing in the prophetic.

Chapter One

GETTING STARTED

WHEN I ASKED GOD TO SPEAK TO ME, I EXPECTED AN EVENT. FIRE from heaven, an angelic choir, or something like that. I never would have thought the first words I would hear from God would have something to do with purchasing a candy bar. But that's exactly how it happened. Over the years, I have really come to appreciate the divine sense of humor. God was being like a Father responding to the request of his eight-year-old son for the gift of a power saw. He laughs a gentle laugh, smiles, and then gives him a small handsaw. His son can still attack a piece of wood, but he's not going to hurt anyone else in the process.

To be sure, I got what I wanted in part—an event. That's how I presented it to you—as a scene from a story. How gracious of the Father, however, to give me an event, as it were, that only under-scored His desire to talk to me about the seemingly small, everyday stuff of life. I got His point loud and clear. No longer was I to look at God's speaking to me as an event or very rare occurrence; no, His speaking would become a normal part of my everyday relationship and communion with Him.

The apostle Paul tells us in Romans 2:11 that God is not a respecter of persons. If He can speak to me about a chocolate bar, then He is able and willing to speak to you, too, about something in your life. If you have struggled with believing He's willing, even desirous, to speak to you, be encouraged. Pick up the Bible and look at the number of unlikely candidates He spoke to from Genesis to Revelation—people like you and I with faults and weaknesses.

He is no respecter of persons; He wants to talk to you about everything, but remember He typically speaks in very simple ways. Now, it's one thing to believe and know that God wants to speak to us personally each and every day. It's quite a different thing to believe He wants to say something to us that is actually to be shared with someone else—in other words, that God wants to use us prophetically to touch the lives of others.

The Lord indicated through Paul that all could prophesy. Paul described it as the gift to be most desired because it builds up the body of Christ (see 1 Cor. 14:1,3,39). That's why the prophetic gift is so great. Prophecy is God's love expressed through ordinary believers in ways that powerfully impact people's lives. It's not complicated, and it's not rocket science. If we can be still and listen for a moment, we can learn to hear and communicate the voice of the Lord to others. The basic foundations are simple enough, and once we understand them, we can spend a lifetime continuing to grow in the gift.

Typically, when I teach on being used of God in the prophetic, people are unsure about God speaking to them for someone else. They really question the Father using them in this way. "Am I prophetic?" is the basic question asked in a number of different ways. Many misconceptions arise because we tend to compare ourselves to the Old Testament (OT) prophets, or we compare ourselves with those today who seem to have had wild prophetic experiences. I love encountering God, and my experiences have their place in my journey, but they do not make me prophetic or equip me to prophesy.

We can make the same mistake I did about how God speaks to us. We can view it as an event rather than a normal part of our everyday lives. We can imagine the event to be an "over the top" supernatural encounter. These experiences may happen to people once in a while, but they aren't the daily norm.

My own journey in the prophetic began initially when I was praying for people. I would receive pictures, simple phrases, or impressions, and I would pray them without prophesying. Sometimes, I would get Bible verses. When I would finish praying for people, they would often ask me how I knew the things I shared with them because they accurately described where they were in their lives.

You may be more prophetic than you think you are, you just haven't refined your "hearing" ability. God wants to touch people in the marketplaces, schools, and homes of our communities, and He is delighted to use us to do so. Though learning to prophesy is just the beginning, just the tip of the iceberg for becoming a prophetic servant, it is the place where we begin our journey. This chapter will deal with how God speaks and how we hear and process what He tells us. While addressing these two points, we will also begin to discuss how we deliver what He gives us in the most edifying way.

How God Speaks

God initiates the whole prophetic process by speaking something to us. Proverbs 20:12 tells us that God has created both the *hearing ear* and the *seeing eye*. He created us as spiritual beings with the ability to hear His voice and see with His eyes. This was Jesus's model. He said that He did what He saw the Father do and said what He heard the Father say (see John 5:19; 12:49). In John 10:3-4, Jesus said that His sheep would know His voice. The world does its best to drown out that still small voice, but if we will dial down and train ourselves to watch and listen, we will learn to hear His voice. The following are ways in which we might hear or perceive prophetic words. It is by no means an exhaustive list, but it is a good place to begin.

Bible Verses

The single most powerful way God will speak to a believer is through His Word. When we eat of His Word, the Bread of Life, we are also storing up a *prophetic bakery* in our inner man out of which the Lord may draw *prophetic bread* to feed others. I have heard people say, "All I ever get for people is Bible verses." That's great—for this is a wonderful way to prophesy! It doesn't get much better than the Living Word giving a *rhema*, a now word, to one of His children.

The Lord may speak a verse to you for someone else, or He may give you the verse with an accompanying encouragement. Often, I find out later that the verse I have given someone is their life verse or the very verse they have been recently reading or praying. Never minimize the power of Scripture to speak to people's lives. I encourage believers to daily pray Scripture. In this way, they build themselves up in the knowledge of God while also storing up an arsenal the Holy Spirit can pull from at any time to minister to one of Abba's children.

Sometimes, you may get a specific Bible reference. Be sure to look it up before giving it as a prophetic word to make sure it says what you think it says. Other times you may get a verse but you can't remember the exact chapter and verse reference. Simply quote the verse as the encouraging word and tell them what book it is in if you know.

Pictures

The phrase, "A picture is worth a thousand words," is very true in prophetic listening. God may speak to you about someone you are to prophesy over by giving you pictures of places or activities through which you will learn to discern a message for that individual. If you are normally a visual processer, the picture may simply be the means God is using to communicate the message to you. It may have nothing to do with the person, but is God's way of getting your attention and defining the word He wants you to speak. Other times, the picture may really be for the person you are prophesying to.

A picture, therefore, may be literal or symbolic. This is where growing in interpretation is necessary. There will be more discussion on this subject later. For now, it is important just to understand this as one of the means by which God speaks.

A Word or Phrase

You may receive a single word such as *hurt, transition,* or *authority.* Or you may receive a phrase such as, *he/she is a singer, called to preach,* or *he's a faithful man.* We are to step out in faith, believing God to give words to fill in the gaps. If we don't receive anything else, we give what we receive. (For example, "I feel like God says you are a faithful man, and He loves that about you.")

Romans 12:6 encourages us to prophesy, if our gift is prophecy, and to do so "in proportion to our faith." As we step out, God will often give more. At the same time, we need to understand that it's not how long or how short a word is that gives it power and impact. Our job is to be obedient to say what God is telling us to say and no more. We're responsible for giving the word to the person as God is prompting us, leaving the outcome in God's hands.

On one occasion, I was praying for people during a ministry time at a church. I saw a particular man and heard the phrase, *tell him I know.* It seemed like such an insignificant word to me. I asked the Lord, "Tell him You know what? Give me more information."

He patiently encouraged me, "Just tell him I know."

I put my hand on the man's shoulder and said to him, "I feel the Lord just says to tell you, 'I know.'" The man collapsed to the floor and began to weep as Abba graciously encouraged his heart about his situation.

Sometimes, all we need to know is that God knows, and it's enough. It's not the length of the word that makes it powerful. We simply learn to give what we receive.

External Circumstances

There are times God may speak to you through external circumstances. Perhaps a person's name, an item of their clothing, or some external activity that is happening around you or them may facilitate a prophetic impulse. I remember one specific time this happened to me.

As I recall, I was in a side room prophesying over a couple on our mission's base while there was construction work taking place in the room next to us. The noise of hammers and saws was very distracting, and I was going to get up to ask them to stop for a few moments until we were finished. Instead, the Lord told me to listen for a moment. As I listened to the sound of the saws, He told me the couple I was praying for was under construction. He was tearing out walls in their hearts to make more room for Him and His plans for them. After I shared this with them, they both confirmed it, telling me that even their physical home was being remodeled. In fact, they said a wall had been taken out in one of their main rooms to make more space.

Similarly, there have been times when the Lord has spoken to me about someone's name in connection with a Bible character of the same name. At other times, He has highlighted a piece of clothing or their shoes to give an aspect of revelation. I have learned to pay attention to my surroundings, and I would encourage you to do the same.

I must give a caution here with external circumstances. Be careful not to become dependent on this type of revelation. It can be easy for some people to find something spiritual about every single circumstance and try to turn it into a prophetic word or spiritual signpost. We need to go beyond just seeing circumstances and learn to listen to God's heart. Over-dependency on outward circumstances and appearances can also lead prophetic people to fall into the trap of trying to *read* people according to outer appearance.

Let's remember the story of David in the Bible. When Samuel went to Jesse's house to anoint Israel's next king, his first impression was that it must be Eliab. Outwardly Eliab was a strong, good-looking young man. God quickly corrected Samuel, reminding him that the Lord doesn't judge by the outward appearance, but He looks at the heart (see 1 Sam. 16). It was the youngest and "least of these" sons, David, who ended up being the one God had chosen.

What we see on the outside may have nothing to do with what God wants to say to us or others. It's important to know that prophetic ministry has nothing to do with *reading* people. This is a soulish practice. *We do not read people.*

Impressions

An impression is like a *knowing* in your inner man. You feel like *you know that you know* something about the person you are ministering to, yet there's no practical reason for you knowing what you know.

For example, there have been times that I had impressions regarding the receiver's parents being missionaries or the person's spouse or child being ill while these individuals were not present at the ministry time. I didn't have a word, or a phrase, or a picture. I just knew because it was impressed on my spirit, so to speak.

An impression may be somewhat faint and undefined, or it may be very clear. If the impression isn't clear, speak to the Lord in your spirit and ask Him questions like, "I'm sensing something, Lord. What are You saying?" Or, "Give me clarity, Lord." We may receive clarity because accompanied with the impression is a picture that confirms or explains the impression, giving further understanding of what God may be saying. This is an impression in your *mind's eye*.

Often when I am traveling, I pray in advance for people or leaders I will be meeting. Prior to one such trip, I was praying for a number of leaders, asking God questions about them and making notes for each one while He was speaking to me. As I prayed for one of them, a woman, I had a strong impression about her daughters, and I didn't even know if she had daughters. I didn't have any distinct information, so I simply wrote *daughters* in the margin of my notes with a question mark next to it and continued down my list. When I finished, I went back to the question mark and began to ask God about these daughters. In the waiting, He gave me a few simple things about them.

After the first session with the group that weekend, one of the leaders came and asked me to pray for her daughters. I went down my list and found this was the one I had written *daughters* next to and was able to prophesy regarding God's heart for these daughters.

If we wait and ask about our impressions, the Lord will lead us. Learning to listen, wait, and obey over time helps develop and draw out with more clarity the impressions we receive.

Emotions

Feelings of joy, compassion, mercy, or grief can come into our hearts as we minister to someone. These can come as a release of the heart of God enabling you to feel what He feels about the person you are ministering to. The gist of the word of the Lord for them is the overflow of the feelings of His heart. This should be followed with an explanation of what you sense the Lord is saying through the expression.

Jeremiah was known as the *weeping prophet*, partly because he prophesied out of God's emotions over the people of Judah and

Jerusalem. This wasn't a manifestation of his own human sympathy and didn't have anything to do with his own emotional bent. In fact, he may have felt nothing prior to prophesying.

I have had times when I was actually feeling tired and dull when suddenly I was overwhelmed by God's compassion over the person I was speaking to and I began to weep. If God speaks to you in this manner, it's important to understand the message behind this expression. Otherwise, the person may be left confused and wondering what might be wrong with you.

Dreams/Visions

God may give you a dream or vision that may relate to you personally, have corporate ramifications, or give prophetic input for an individual prophetic ministry time. God may give you a dream that you are ministering or prophesying over someone. It can be vague, where you will pray for someone, or it can be specific like you are praying for someone named Mary. This is a tricky area and should be approached with much discernment. Factors to consider here have to do with whether or not the dream is literal or symbolic, what the timing of the dream is, and whether it is for you personally or for the body.

For me, most of my non-personal dreams are for intercession. When I have dreams about nations, they are often to give me revelation for prayer. Many of my dreams are either encouragements or warnings to pray for people, some whom I know and some I don't.

There are a number of good books on dream interpretation, so I will not go into detail on this subject. My only input is to help you understand that when it comes to methods of interpretation there is no *one size fits all*. Many people will favor a book or a method and force every dream they have or every dream they interpret for others into that method. We would do well to remember dreams are a language and God wants us to develop our own vocabularies with Him as He gives us insight into interpretation.

The way He speaks to me will be different than the way He speaks to you. I grew up with dogs as pets, and all my life I have always had a dog. Maybe you, on the other hand, have had nothing but bad experiences with dogs all your life. The way I might interpret the presence of a dog in my dream could be completely different than the way you would see it. While there are good basic interpretive tools to help us grow, at the end of the day, the Lord hides a matter so we can search it out (see Prov. 25:2). Dreams are designed to bring us near His heart and to cause us to seek His face. The same is true of visions.

Visions can be brief pictures in our minds that combine images with impressions or full-on encounters where we feel like we are there. Like dreams, visions can be given to inspire us to pray. They can also be given to prepare us for something or someone we will be connected to in ministry. The purpose with both, in connection with prophetic ministry, is to bring strength, edification, and encouragement to the body of Christ.

One of the most difficult things in understanding dreams and visions as related to prophetic ministry is interpretation—whether they're to be taken literally or symbolically and whether their timing is for now or some day in the future. I have known people who got into trouble because they misread the timing of a dream and stepped into something too quickly.

I have been recording my dreams for twenty-five years, and I am often amazed to find that I may have just started walking into the fulfillment of something I dreamed about five years ago. This particular area of the prophetic, especially as it relates to a corporate people, really needs to be prayed through and shared with leaders before any major steps are taken or decisions made.

It's also good to understand that dreams and visions aren't signs of spiritual maturity. If we pursue dreams and/or visions because we think they will make us more spiritual, give us more recognition, or enhance our prophetic position, then we are missing the point. The Father loves to give us gifts and blessings in the Holy Spirit, because He loves us. His desire is for us to take them and use them for the edification of His Bride.

These are just a few of the ways God may speak, and this list is in no way exhaustive. It's a good place to start, though. Anyone who is serious about growing in his or her prophetic gifting should pray about learning to listen and pay attention.

HOW WE HEAR GOD AND PROCESS HIS MESSAGE

Okay, so God speaks in a lot of different ways in the normal course of everyday life. But the question begs answering—"How can I know He is speaking to me?" Or better yet, "How do I hear Him?"

Some people don't think they can hear God speak to them. I have been told frequently by various individuals that they just don't hear God. They ask for words, but they don't get anything. There are two things I address in response to their experiences.

My first suggestion is to dial down and not try so hard. Instead of struggling to receive a gift and get a word, think of prophecy as an extension of your vertical prayer life with God. In your fellowship with God, He talks and you listen, and you talk and He listens. You don't have to struggle and strain to talk to Him and receive from Him. Speaking and listening are ever changing and growing parts of your fellowship and communion with God. Prophesying is an extension of that relationship. You are just adding a horizontal dimension to the process of prayer. A third participant is brought into the conversation with you and God. Think of it as a three-way conversation.

The second suggestion is to ask God specific questions. Some people don't hear from God because they ask in such a general way they wouldn't recognize the answer if it came to them. We can say, "Speak to me, God."

He might answer, "Which of the hundred billion pieces of information that are constantly before Me would you like Me to tell you?"

There are times I receive immediate words or impressions for people, but often words come in response to *specific* questions. I have five children, and when it comes to them expressing their desires to me, there is nothing general about it. If one of them wants ten dollars for some kind of activity, they don't come to me and say, "Dad, I am imagining an unspecified need for an unde-fined activity. Can you help me out?" Or if they would like me to help one of their friends with a ride to and from somewhere, they don't say, "Dad, there is a teenager somewhere on the face of the earth who needs to be transported from point A to point B. What do you think?" In my house, it sounds more like, "Dad, can I have ten dollars for a movie?" Or, "Dad, can you give my friend a ride home?"

When I am ministering, I may receive the impression that I am to prophesy over someone before I know what it is I am supposed to say. So I begin to ask God some questions. "Who is this person to You, God? How do You want to encourage her today?" Having a few questions in the back of your mind to ask God about those you may end up ministering to is helpful.

A few years ago, I was ministering in Poland. One of the cool things about learning to prophesy from relationship is that min-istry doesn't depend on how you feel. I flew from Kansas City to Chicago to Amsterdam to Warsaw. I caught a couple hours rest in Warsaw and then took a three-hour train ride from Warsaw to Gli-wice. Though my body was tired, my mind wouldn't shut off. I was to speak on the prophetic to a group of Charismatic Catholics the following evening, so I grabbed my notebook to review my notes. There was an English-speaking Polish woman in her mid-thirties sitting next to me. As I pulled my notebook from my backpack, I heard that familiar whisper from Abba, "Prophesy."

Feeling pretty tired and having no immediate impressions, I opened my notebook to some blank pages and began a conversation with God about this woman. I asked questions like, "What is her life's dream? What is she good at? What does she think about how You see her?" As the Lord responded to my questions with impressions, pictures, and words, I made notes. Ten minutes and three pages later, I was ready to go, tired or not.

I introduced myself to her as a believer in Jesus who often gets impressions from Him for other people and told her He had given me some impressions for her. I asked her if she would like to know them. She had been watching me make all my notes and asked, "Is all that about me?" I told her that it was, that God really liked her and had a lot to say.

Over the next several minutes, I was able to share God's heart and dream for her, accurately touching on several relevant areas of her life. She didn't receive the Lord but was on the verge of tears a couple of times as God touched some tender areas in her heart. Her stop came up and as she was leaving she said, "I always thought God was way out there somewhere and that He didn't really care about me or the details of my life. I didn't know He cared about me and was so close." On an evangelism scale of one to ten, that encounter moved her up several notches, opening her heart to the gospel—all because I asked God a few questions about her.

ASK SPECIFIC QUESTIONS

Specific questions usually bring specific answers or results. When I am doing training seminars, I will often bring two or three people up to the front and give the rest of the attendees three questions to ask God about each of the ones I have brought forward. It's fun to watch the people, many of whom have never prophesied before, receive specific answers to the questions they ask and then accurately prophesy.

The following is a list of topics and correlating questions I typically ask God before or during a prophetic ministry time. You can use these or come up with some of your own.

What are their spiritual gifts?

We aren't asking just to know their gifts, but also the context in which gifts fit into their overall calling and the expression of Christ through them.

What are their motivational/service gifts?

(Note: some gifts overlap in multiple categories.) Again, as we ask about gifts, we are considering gifts in the scheme of their destiny.

Are there characteristics related to five-fold callings?

Not everyone is going to fit in here, but there are a couple of applications. They may not be called as an apostle, but the Lord may want to highlight some apostolic characteristics (church planting, for example) that they carry. Another thing to keep in mind here is that some apostolic characteristics may apply to the marketplace and don't have to find their expression within the walls of a church. A person might carry certain aspects of these gifts but not necessarily be vocationally called to the respective office. We need to practice listening skills in these areas and not speak out too soon, calling people out as apostles and prophets just because we sense a type of gifting that relates to the offices.

Ultimately, it's God who calls and sets apart individuals to any of the five-fold ministries. Our prophetic words can't create or open a door to these offices; they can only confirm them. We must exercise caution here. I believe we can do a disservice to a young person to call them out as a prophet or apostle ahead of God's timing. In essence, we paint a target on them for the enemy. If they aren't mature enough to handle it, pride can rise up to cause them to move out too quickly, and they may try to bypass the training ground God sets in place for those called to these offices. That is one reason to identify the characteristics without necessarily applying the office. You can read Romans 12, First Corinthians 12, Ephesians 4, and First 1 Peter 4 to gain further insight on the categories of spiritual gifts.

Is God highlighting a parallel biblical character?

Is there someone whom they be might be like in character, calling, or gifting?

What about their prophetic history?

Are there some past prophetic words, promises, or visitations that relate to what God wants to say now? What might He be adding to that, or expanding on, in relation to those past experiences?

Is God saying something in connection with their family line or inheritance?

Is there something in the family line that God wants to highlight, bless, or activate?

Ask God about their prayer journal/life scriptures.

What is the cry of their heart to the Lord? What have they written down? What scriptures has God been speaking to them through?

Is God speaking about their season of life?

What type of season are they facing? Are they in the desert? Coming out of the desert? Beginning a new season? In a time of healing and restoration, or soaring and taking ground? What is the Lord speaking to them in their current season?

Other Questions

- If Jesus was standing in front of them right now, what would He say to them?

- What is whispered about them before the throne of the Lord?

- What is their reputation before heaven and men?

- How do they affect the different rooms they enter?

- What does the Lord say about how they bless Him?

- What does God want to say about their family (present or not)?

These are all ways to connect our hearts to God for an individual we are ministering to. God probably won't answer all the questions, but He will answer the ones that are on His heart for the person at the moment. Don't linger too long over any question. When I am praying over this list, I don't usually labor for more than a minute on each question, unless God begins to speak to me about it. This is a good way to grow in hearing His voice in specific ways. You can ask God to speak to you while you sit in church, in an office, at work, or anywhere really. Keep a pad handy, and write down what He tells you. Then ask the person if you can share your *God impressions* with them. Just be sure to deliver your words with kindness. This is a very safe way to begin prophesying because there is no pressure to come up with a word on the spot. You have already heard, now you are just delivering the message!

GETTING PLUGGED IN

1. Now that you have read this chapter, can you pinpoint times you actually heard God's voice without realizing it?

2. Review the different ways God speaks. Highlight the particular ways He speaks to you. Ask Him to increase both your hearing and understanding of those ways. Ask God to help you listen and hear in these new ways.

3. Choose an arena to practice listening and prophesying. This could be work, church, home group, family, or some other setting. The next time you are in that setting, ask the Lord to impress on you someone to prophesy over. Then choose a few questions to ask God about them. Write down the things you feel the Lord is saying to them, and when you have the opportunity, ask them if you can share your God impressions. If you want, you can tell them you are practicing listening to God, and you would like to practice on them, if it's okay. It's good to remember that *the heart of New Testament (NT) prophecy is strength, edification, and encouragement, so be extremely careful with specific directional words, and avoid judgmental words that point out faults, weaknesses, and sins.* Don't declare your word over them as if you are the sovereign mouthpiece of God, but rather submit your word in a spirit of gentleness so they can feel the freedom to discern and weigh it.

Chapter Two

NAVIGATING THROUGH A WORD

How do we hear, understand, and release a prophetic word? There are three simple components involved in the process. If you have ever prophesied, you probably walked through them without even thinking about it.

First, *God speaks*. Second, *we hear and discern*. Third, *we give expression to what we have heard and discerned*. These components all flow together to give the sum of a prophetic word. This can sound a little technical or complicated, so before I explain, let me share a few things about navigating through prophetic revelation.

The gift of prophecy is meant to flow from the heart of God to the heart of the Bride. It's not some mysterious process that happens in a vacuum, but rather it's meant to pour out of our ongoing relationship and conversation with God. I see the development of the prophetic gifting in a believer's life as an extension of the nurturing of their own personal relationship with Jesus. In this light, prophecy becomes an expanded conversation I have with

God about someone He loves and wants to speak to. It's not some cut and dry, black and white, turn it on/turn it off process. I don't put on my prophecy hat when it's time to prophesy and take it off when I finish. It's a growing process. Along the journey, we are allowed to ask questions and talk to God as we would in our personal dialogue with Him.

THE PROPHETIC PROCESS

Prophecy begins with God speaking to us. As we have learned already, it may come as an impression, picture, phrase, or other form of communication from God in order to strengthen someone else. What comes from God is clean, pure, and right. It's what is on His heart for the person we are prophesying to. In this stage, it may come as a crystal clear message, a faint impression, or a simple word or phrase. In its essence, it's a reflection of God's love and desire for the person to whom we are prophesying.

Remember, we should only speak what we hear Abba say. Discernment is key in our understanding revelation. Here, there will always be more room for growth. When we are new in the gift and are learning how to filter God's words through our own paradigms, weaknesses, and limited scriptural knowledge, we will often come short of delivering that pure word of God without putting our own understanding or spin on it. We may end up only rightly expressing 10 percent of what began as that pure word from God. I believe this is why, in His wisdom, He calls us to prophesy things that strengthen, edify, and encourage the body of Christ (see 1 Cor. 14:3-5). If our heart's desire is truly to bless others, and our words are ordered that way, then even if we miss it a little bit, we are still bringing encouragement. This is also why Paul admonished believers to test prophetic words and keep the good (see 1 Thess. 5:19-22).

Believers are commanded to weigh prophetic words and not just believe everything anyone prophesies or prays over them without practicing discernment. We will discuss this further a little later, but the point is no one comes out of the blocks a complete, mature, prophetic vessel. We are all immature when we first practice the gift. The good news is we all can grow up and become mature prophetic servants.

One of the best ways to mature in interpreting prophetic words is to dialogue with God during the prophetic process. Often, this means asking Him questions. The whole idea of asking questions and having prophetic conversation is quite scriptural and was one of the ways the biblical prophets connected with God. In many of their encounters, they asked questions of God or angels to gain clarity (see Jer. 14:7-9; Zech. 5:5-11). Sometimes, God or angels asked the prophets questions to prepare their hearts to receive what was to follow (see Isa. 6:8-9; Jer. 1:11-14; Ezek. 37:1-4; Rev. 7:13-14). Having the dialogue with God over prophetic words is one of the ways we gain insight into learning interpretive skills. In some cases, the interpretation is very simple and plain and no questions need to be asked, while other times it is more sensitive or complex.

I recall a time when I walked into the prayer room at IHOP-KC one day and saw one of my friends pacing and praying. I immediately received the phrase, *I am saving the best for her*. It didn't seem like a big deal, but I walked over and shared the phrase with her. It was the answer to the very question she had just asked God about. The interpretation in this case was clear and easy to understand.

In other cases, the interpretation isn't as easy to discern. This is especially true when the Lord shows you a picture, gives you an impression, or highlights a single word that can have multiple implications. *Music* is one such word. You may hear or have an impression of music over or around a person. This could mean that they are a musician or worshiper or singer. It could also mean that God is singing a new song over their lives (see Song of Sol. 2:12), where Jesus refers to the return of the season of singing. It might also have to do with the music their life makes before the Lord as the symphony of their heart unfolds in worship. Maybe they work in a music store. How we interpret this makes a difference in how we express the word to the person as we deliver it.

I have had times where I absolutely knew the person was a musician and the Lord was setting him apart in worship. I have also had the strong impression of music over someone without a clear connection as to how it related to her life at the moment. This is where we hold conversation with God. "How does this apply, Lord?" we may need to ask. It's okay to ask and wait and listen as the process unfolds.

Pictures may be even more difficult to interpret. God speaks prophetically to people through pictures—sometimes in a single frame, sometimes in multiple frames. This doesn't mean we always need to tell the person the picture in great detail or even tell it at all. The picture may simply be a communicative device God is using to formulate the message inside us. On the other hand, the picture may be strictly for them, without making sense to us at all. Again, we can ask questions in the process to help us discern what to share and what not to share.

I had a highly prophetic young man on one of my prophecy teams. After a time of watching my team in action without being allowed to prophesy, he was finally released to begin giving words. The first time he was released to prophesy, he spoke to the recipient seated in front of us and said something like, "I see you in a coffin, and the lid is closed." In the IHOP-KC prophecy rooms, we go out of our way to let people know we are moving in the *gift* of prophecy, not the *office* of prophet. Still, some people have been a part of a culture of believing those prophesying are really prophets. I think the man who was receiving ministry may have held such a view because the look on his face reflected, "The prophet says I'm going to die!" Inwardly, I really felt for the poor man, and I wasn't too thrilled that the young man on my team had launched such a word his first time out! But, somehow, I decided to ride it out.

The other members of the team had words for the gentleman regarding the resurrection of old dreams and the Lord restoring him as he was coming out of a season of dying to himself into a season of new life. In light of the other words given to the man, I could see that the picture the young man received was accurate regarding what was happening in the gentleman's life, but my young friend didn't take the time to ask how the picture was to be applied in giving his word. In this case, the receiver didn't need to know about the picture. The picture was the way God conveyed the message to the young man, and had he asked the Lord a few questions, he would have understood that.

After the ministry was over, I brought a slight word of correction and encouragement, and the young man went on to grow greatly in his gifting. I have found a few questions to be particularly helpful in this process. The first is, "Lord, is this picture for them, or is it for me?" Mostly, I automatically know; however, this knowledge will increase as you gain experience in prophesying. Sometimes, I don't automatically know, so the question helps me gain clarity. Generally, the way I know depends on how the Lord answers. When He doesn't give me further information, the picture is sometimes for them.

One day, for example, I was prophesying over a lady, and I had a clear picture of her wearing a major league baseball catcher's uniform. She was behind the plate, playing in a game. It seemed like an odd picture and made no sense to me at all. I asked the Lord, "What does this mean?" He didn't answer, even after I asked a few times. I knew the picture was from Him, but He wasn't divulging any further information.

After a few minutes of arguing with Him about it, I decided to just tell her what I saw. I told her it didn't make any sense to me, but I saw her as a catcher in a baseball game, and I thought maybe the Lord was telling her that she was learning to receive well from Him. She began to laugh, so I asked her why. She related to me that she had been in our prayer room that morning, and the Lord had given her a picture of herself standing in the batter's box in a base-ball game, and He told her to stay in the game. She said, "Lord, if this is You, when I go into the prophecy rooms this afternoon, have someone give me a picture about baseball." The picture was for her, and I didn't need to know anything else. There was noth-ing for me to add. It was His playful answer to her earlier question, and I was the available vessel to bring the picture.

I have had other similar experiences where I didn't under-stand the meaning of the picture that I was simply supposed to give. At times, they have been descriptions of literal places the per-son is familiar with. Other times, they have had a clearer spiritual application. This is the case with about 5 percent of the pictures I receive. The other 95 percent of the time, the picture is the com-munication tool through which God speaks to me. There is no science to it, which is why God wants us to engage Him in the pro-phetic conversation and ask Him questions.

Additionally, I encourage you to get feedback when you give pictures to people without any accompanying word or exhortation. If you give ten people pictures and nothing else, and ten people tell you that your pictures make absolutely no sense to them, then it's time to stop giving them for a while. It doesn't mean you are hearing incorrectly; the problem could be in the interpretive stage. Have some conversations with God on the subject and try practic-ing prophecy without giving pictures for a time to sharpen your listening skills. If we stay with the process and remain teachable, the Lord will help us. As we gain experience, the process becomes more natural.

Is it important to tell the person about the picture we received? The determining factor is the answer to this question, "What will bring the most edification to the person receiving the word?" If sharing the picture helps, I share it. If it doesn't add anything, I don't. We learn these things as we grow in our experience of prophesying.

Another area where inquiring of God is helpful is with impressions. I previously described an impression as an *inner knowing*. You may not yet have words to go with the impression, but you know something is up. Perhaps, you have the concept in your spirit, but you are waiting for the words to catch up. It's like God is pulling it out of you as you are pulling on Him. Little prayers like, "Help me see, Lord," or, "What are You saying, Lord?" are helpful as we wait and listen. In this way, we gain clarity and can release the word.

This area of discerning the word of the Lord is always the trickiest, and we should understand as we grow here we will likely make some mistakes. Don't cover them up or over-spiritualize them to mean something else. Hold yourself accountable and jump back into the conversation with God. If we ask Him lots of questions and humble ourselves, we will grow. Remember that the heart of NT prophecy is strength, edification, and encouragement. If we make that our goal, even if we miss a little while we are learning, we won't hurt anyone.

I remember a story about three young ladies who were connected with our fellowship. They went out to dinner and decided to prophesy over their waitress. As they each prophesied, the waitress began to weep. All this took place in the course of her serving them at their table. When the group was ready to leave, they asked the waitress which of their prophetic words really touched her. She told them that none of them did, and for the most part they were inaccurate. When they asked her why she wept, she said she could feel such love and concern coming from them that it moved her heart and caused her to cry.

You see, when our hearts are in the right place, we will learn from such examples, and our humility and "teachableness" will keep us on track as we learn from our mistakes and grow. On the other hand, people can be so afraid they are going to make a mistake that they never prophesy. The only way to grow in prophetic gifting is to prophesy.

OUR EXPRESSION

The prophetic process culminates in our prophesying what we have heard and discerned God to say. We hear something from God, we discern it, and then we prophesy. But how do we pass it on?

The key to answering this question is in First Corinthians 14:3, where Paul says prophecy should strengthen, edify, and encourage the Church. We want to deliver what God has spoken in the way that will edify and strengthen most the one to whom we are prophesying. Three things to consider here are delivery style (how do we say it?), quantity (how much do we say?), and the gist of the message (how do we make the message clear?).

How Do We Say It?

It's good to develop a comfortable approach in how to begin prophesying over people in different settings. Generally speaking, we want to learn to be *naturally supernatural,* giving words in simple ways that people can receive without a lot of religious jargon or attachment. Jesus is our model here. If you follow the gospel narratives, you will find that Jesus personally prophesied to several people. His words were simple, clear, and to the point with great regard for the dignity and heart of the person He was addressing. He said what He heard the Father say.

In your delivery, unless very clearly directed by the Lord, avoid odd or bizarre types of deliveries accompanied with strange physical motions. Some people think this makes the word more mystical and spiritual. While there might be an occasion where God wants to accompany a word with a seemingly strange physical manifestation, for the most part He will speak to people in ways they can receive. Even physical expressions of the prophetic in Scripture were tied to everyday things. Jeremiah prophesied from the potter's house things that Israel would understand (see Jer. 18). Jesus told parables about fishing and farming.

Once in a while, the Lord may clearly direct us to do an action of some sort, but that doesn't mean it's supposed to be the norm. For example, I was praying for a young man once, and the Lord told me to pick him up, give him a bear hug, tussle his hair, and then tell him, "This is how the Father feels about you." You can imagine my hesitancy, but I obeyed the Lord. The young man began to weep as the affections of Abba overwhelmed him. He had never had a father who expressed tender physical affirmation and affection, and his understanding of the fatherhood of God shifted in that moment. This was the one-out-of-a-hundred experience for me, and not the norm. For the most part, we are to deliver the message with tenderness and humility, considering the dignity of the person in each and every prophetic setting.

Prophetic ministry with unbelievers will also call for a different approach. One of my greatest joys is prophesying over unbelievers in secular settings. I have prophesied over people on trains and planes, in restaurants and business offices. I believe people want to know what God thinks about them. They want to believe there is more than what their five senses tell them. There is a spiritual hunger inside people that longs for affirmation, purpose, and love. As I told you in chapter one, when prophesying in such situations, I usually say something like, "Hi, I am a believer in Jesus, and sometimes He gives me impressions about people. Can I share with you some impressions He has given me about you?" So far, no one has told me *no*. One of my friends tells people she is trying to learn to hear God's voice and asks people if she can practice on them. It's good to develop a comfortable way to introduce the prophetic to them.

One thing to keep in mind in these settings is to speak in language people will understand. Forget your *Christianese,* and use words they will understand. If you tell them you see them as *washed in the blood,* they might scream and run out of the room! Check your religious language at the door.

Often, these encounters will lead to good opportunities to share the gospel. During one of my stints in the marketplace, I worked for a pest control company. God was giving me favor with many employees and was using me in both prophecy and healing. I came into the office one day, and one of the secretaries mentioned she had a headache. I offered to pray for her, and the Lord healed her. I came in the next day, and she asked me to lay hands on the copy machine and heal it because it wasn't working!

On another occasion, a receptionist asked me to ask God for a word for her. I said I would and told her to check with me on her lunch break. She came to my desk at lunchtime and asked if God had told me anything. Her countenance was sad, and she said, "He's mad at me, isn't He?"

The Lord had given me just one sentence for her, "Tell her I miss her." I responded, "No, He's not mad at you. He said to tell you that He misses you."

She began to weep. She had been raised in a Christian home but had backslidden and become involved in some dark things. She wanted to return to the Lord but was filled with shame and condemnation, imagining the Lord was angry and wouldn't forgive her. The simple word the Lord had for her comforted her heart and opened the door for me to share the gospel with her and pray for her to return to the Lord.

The Lord loves to set up divine appointments like these. I encourage people in such settings to find a natural approach that works for them. The first few times may seem awkward, but it will get easier as we get used to hearing God's whispers and sharing them with people. Simple openings like, "I have this impression..." or, "I sense the Lord may be saying..." are good ways to begin.

I recommend avoiding the phrase, "Thus saith the Lord." The reason for this is when we say, "Thus saith the Lord," we imply every single word we are saying is 100 percent God-inspired and straight from His mouth. This removes from the receiver the ability to judge the word for himself. He either has to say it's all from God, or none of it's from God.

The apostle Paul said in First Thessalonians 5:19-21 that we are not to despise prophesying or put out the Spirit's fire, but we are to prove all things and hold fast to that which is good. First Corinthians 14:29-33 also demonstrates this when it calls on prophets to judge and weigh the words of others. Both references challenge the Church (corporate and individual) to practice discernment in receiving and applying prophetic words. When a prophetic word is from the Lord, others will bear witness with it in their hearts whether you add, "Thus saith the Lord," or not. Likewise, if it's way off, adding that expression doesn't make it legitimate. There must be room for the receiver to weigh it and prove it.

This isn't to call into question the character of the person delivering the word; it just means that, no matter how mature or immature the vessel delivering the word is, we still have the responsibility to weigh and discern it. Some of the word may immediately apply, some may apply later, and some may never apply. We hold fast to the good and move on. When you eat a piece of fish, if you come to a bone, you don't throw out the whole fish. You pull out the bone and continue eating. We want to give the receiver the opportunity to remove the bones while eating the rest of the fish.

How Much Do We Say?

Once we know what to say, we have to determine how much we say. Again, the answer here rests on what will be the most edifying and encouraging to the receiver.

One aspect to consider is how to clearly give to them the end result of what God has given us. I might get three or four pictures to emphasize one single component of a prophetic word. Is it important that they know every single picture? We don't want the gist of the message to get lost in our explanation of all the pictures and impressions we had in formulating the message. What I saw or felt is only important if it effectively clarifies the message.

I have heard people go into so much detail on what they saw or felt that the message was almost lost in the process. Often, individuals do this to appear more prophetic. They think if they share great pictures or visions or impressions that it will lend more credence to the message. The bottom line comes down to what most edifies the receiver. This goes back to having that conversation with the Holy Spirit while we are prophesying so we can share what He wants in the most effective way.

Avoid processing prophetic words outwardly. Don't say, "I'm getting this picture, followed by this impression and these feelings, and maybe this means this and this means that, etc." We formulate and process inwardly; then, we give the word outwardly.

Another aspect for consideration here goes to how we communicate sensitive information. I am not looking for darkness or wounding when I prophesy, but sometimes it's hard not to pick things up. I have prophesied to people at times and have known there was a particular sin or area they were involved in and that it was holding them back. Other times, I have known there were areas of deep wounding and pain. Keep in mind that the prophetic ministry may involve teams that are prophesying over two to four people at a time. Calling out an individual's sin or their source of pain in this setting could be devastating and humiliating. We must ask why the Lord is showing us these things. His purpose isn't to embarrass and expose people. He wants them to overcome and get healed.

So here is my personal practice concerning such things. When I get revelation of a person's sin, I try to think in terms of redemption and destiny. I ask the Lord about His destiny and calling over the person and who they are to Him. Jesus isn't defining the person by their sin. He is defining them by His love and His purpose for them. People who are stuck in sin have usually lost sight of that and have given up or are stuck on the merry-go-round of guilt, condemnation, and accusation. In these circumstances, I listen for the redemptive information He wants to give me. If I am prophesying over a young man who I strongly sense is involved in pornography or immorality, I ask the Lord about His future and calling. I will emphasize the calling and desire God has for the young man while at the same time speaking to him of the season of consecration and sanctification God desires to take him through to get him there. He leaves the room encouraged that God hasn't quit on him, while at the same time knowing that God wants him to stop sinning and pursue holiness.

The same is true when I receive revelation about someone's wounds. I have had downloads at times about an individual's brokenness. Perhaps they have been abused in some way. Instead of saying, "I see you have been sexually molested by a relative over a period of time," which would bring shame and embarrassment, I ask the Lord what He wants to say that will bring healing and redemption. The Holy Spirit is really good at knowing just what to say to bring restoration without bringing shame and embarrassment.

One of the most powerful words I had for a person was something to the effect that, "I feel the Lord is saying that it's not your fault, and He is fully in love with you and is casting the accuser far from you. He sees you as His pure, spotless Bride." The person began to weep as accusation and shame were broken off. She knew what God was putting His finger on, and it brought significant healing to her. I didn't need to label the type of pain or tell all the details of it.

With these two examples, I'm not saying there isn't a place for further ministry in both types of situations I described. The young man caught up in a particular sin may need to have someone in a private setting come alongside to confront and help him overcome. The person who has been deeply wounded may need further ministry to fully walk out her healing. In both situations, the prophetic word is the launching pad to let them know God knows where they are and He is on their side.

In local church settings, the responses may be different depending on relationships and counseling ministries that may be in place. In IHOP-KC prophecy rooms, most ministry takes place with visitors, so knowing how much to say and how to say it comes more into play. I would still say in any setting that strength, edification, and encouragement should always lead us in the direction of God's redemptive purposes for those we prophesy over.

How Do We Make the Message Clear?

The last thing to consider in expression is how to communicate the content. This has to do with clearly communicating the message we have received. Often, this will be quite simple and straightforward. We have heard something, we have interpreted something, and now we simply say it. It doesn't require a lot of flash, volume, or frills. We share with them what the Lord has shared with us.

I do find, however, that a word may come progressively in stages as I am prophesying, so I am wrapping up one thought while beginning to process another. Sometimes, for the sake of the receiver and myself, I'll ask a clarifying question. All of us are fallible. We are all capable of missing it sometimes. When I receive words that could be potentially confusing or painful if they are off even a little bit, I like to ask questions. I'm not fishing for information I don't have in order to prophesy. I am confirming revelation I do have so I can release it in the most effective way.

For example, one day I was prophesying to a woman in a prophecy room; I was in midstream when the Lord whispered in my ear that she had a son with a learning disability. When we hear something like that from the Lord, we should ask Him why He is telling us this. The information in itself would not have been helpful to the woman if I didn't have context to present it in. I asked, and the Lord responded that He would be this young man's protector and would be his best friend all his life. My impression was that this was a boy of eight or nine years of age. I finished my current thought and asked her, "Do you have a son that is eight or nine?" She told me she did. I then asked if he had a learning disability, and she replied that he did and told me his condition. I shared with her the promise the Lord was making to this young man, which was greatly encouraging to her. While I was sharing this, the Lord whispered one more thing to me. He said, "Tell her his condition is not her fault." She began to weep as the Lord lifted the burden for the responsibility of his condition being on her. Any parent would understand this. We carry the weight of anything that happens to our children, whether we are responsible or not.

So in her case, I heard something from God, I discerned what He was saying, and I was pretty sure of the expression. But why did I ask the questions? None of us are infallible. If I missed it, I could have prophesied for five minutes about her child with a learning disability only to have her say, "I have a daughter, and she is an A-student in a program for the academically gifted." She would have been confused and not edified at all. On the other hand, the fact that I asked the question took nothing away from the powerful effect the word had on her life.

Often when I am prophesying over people, I will hear words about their spouse, their children, or their friends, once in a while even by name. Before I launch into a prophetic word about someone's daughter and her current situation or life calling, I first like to ask, "Do you have a daughter?" Their affirmation to that question generally confirms that I have heard correctly, and then I continue to prophesy.

What happens if they say *no*? I simply say, "Okay," and move on. Better to enter back into the dialogue with God than prophesy wrongly!

Sometimes, revelation comes progressively as we are prophesying, so it's an ongoing process of learning to carry on a conversation with the Holy Spirit and the receiver at the same time. I want to emphasize again that, in these situations, we are not fishing for information we don't have. We are clarifying the picture or impression to bring the most edification to the receiver.

Another thing to note in delivering the content is that a prophetic word doesn't have to be long and wordy to be powerful. As previously mentioned, sometimes less is more. If the prophetic word is not recorded or written down, people can tend to forget a lengthy word. Length and wordiness don't make it any more or less spiritual or powerful. At the end of the day, the final answer to the question of how we say what we say comes back to the question of what will bring the most edification to the receiver.

GETTING PLUGGED IN

1. What is the foundational question to ask regarding how and what to say in giving a prophetic word?

2. Out of the three parts of the prophetic process, what area do you feel the strongest in? What area do you need the most improvement in?

3. Do any of the areas seem intimidating to you? Why?

4. What do you think you can do to improve in all these areas?

Chapter Three

ADDITIONAL INSTRUCTION AND ENCOURAGEMENT

As the title indicates, this is somewhat of a wrap-it-up chapter. Here you will find some things to keep in mind in giving, receiving, and stewarding prophetic words as you grow in your journey. Understanding the gift of prophecy and beginning to step out are only the start. The gift shouldn't be viewed as a project to be conquered before moving on to another spiritual mountain. It is a living, evolving gift because it connects us to the heart of the Father and there are always new things to learn on the journey.

After years of personal and corporate prophetic ministry, I am still learning things that increase my ability and joy in prophetic ministry. Some of them come in the continuing act of prophesying, and some come from observation and personal encounter with Christ. I encourage you to go forward with a wide-open heart. The rest of this chapter is full of helps to do that.

STEWARDING PROPHETIC WORDS

I highly encourage you to keep a prophetic journal containing all your prophetic words, encounters, and dreams and visions. I have been doing this for over twenty years and have found this practice to be helpful on several levels.

First, it brings encouragement and strength when I review the journal and see how many of my words or dreams have come to pass or are in the process of unfolding in the moment. It also helps me measure my growth in the realm of the prophetic as I see the progression of how I have learned to hear more clearly and how my heart has been enlarged to perceive things from God. I consider this a vital part of stewarding the prophetic information the Lord gives me.

I went through a season where I was dreaming very little. When I asked the Lord about it, He asked me if I remembered my last few dreams and if I had written them down. I had not and told Him so. He said that if I wasn't going to steward them wisely, then He wasn't going to give them to me. I pretty much write down everything now, if I have the slightest inkling it might be God.

How do we steward the prophetic words we receive besides writing them down? There are two things to keep in mind here. First, we have to learn how to discern and receive a word in the moment, and then, we need to understand what to do with it once we have embraced it.

How do we discern prophetic words spoken over us? Some people take everything prophesied over them as the gospel, swallowing it hook, line, and sinker. Others think that just because something was prophesied it will automatically come to pass. Still others take only the parts of a word that immediately apply and throw everything else away. There are three things that every believer should do when they receive a prophetic word.

Testing a Word

A word must be weighed or judged. Again, as Paul said in First Thessalonians 5:19-21, we do not despise prophecies, but we do test them and keep what is good. Not every thought that comes to people's minds is from God, neither is every prophetic word from Him. People are often afraid to offend someone prophesying over them, so instead of weighing their prophetic words and holding the one prophesying accountable when they miss it, they take in everything.

Personally, I want to know if I have prophesied wrongly. I am only human, and no matter how gifted I am, I can miss it. There are circumstances in ministry that can deplete my ability to hear and feel the heart of God. If I am extremely tired or emotionally exhausted, I know I am more susceptible to missing it. I have to watch myself in ministry situations and know what my limitations are so I don't move beyond my physical, spiritual, and emotional capacities. I want to and need to be held accountable for what I prophesy.

By the same token, I weigh prophetic words that are spoken over me. Paul states that it is our responsibility to test prophetic words and to hold fast to the good.

There are two steps involved in testing a prophetic word. First, a true prophetic word should conform to Scripture. This doesn't mean it has to be Scripture or contain a lot of Scripture, but it shouldn't violate basic scriptural principles. It should not discount Scripture or supersede Scripture. If a word calls you to do something that is not in line with biblical practice or doctrine, it should be rejected immediately.

Second, a true prophetic word should bear witness with your own spirit. The apostle John says all believers have an anointing that teaches them discernment. More specifically, he says in First John 2:27 that the anointing abides in us and instructs us in all things.

The witness I speak of may manifest itself in different people in different ways. The gist of it is that we have the inner peace of God regarding the word. It may be confirmed by our current circumstances, by other words, or by things the Lord is speaking to us inwardly. In some way, the word bears witness with the anointing in us that the word is of and from God. It may address or call us to something we are not yet even familiar with, but something on the inside says *yes*. That's the important thing to know when testing a word for validity.

I have personally experienced this with particular words I have received in the past. There has been a grace on me over the years to sustain a prayer life and intercession. Intercession has always been a natural outgrowth of my pursuit of God's heart. Still, it took me many years to realize and embrace my calling as an intercessory missionary. During those years, I served in various ministerial capacities but always found the time and place for intercession.

At one point in my life when I was contemplating stepping back into pastoral ministry, I was in a meeting where a prophetic man was ministering. He himself had a prayer ministry whereby he traveled to different places in the earth to pray over geographic regions. He called me out and prophesied over me. I stood up, and he began to speak to me of a calling to the ministry of prayer. It was so impactful to me spiritually that I was literally knocked to the ground at the hearing of the word, an experience that has only happened to me a few times. Yet even as I was going down, I was thinking, *No, Lord, I want to pastor again!* I struggled inside myself, my spirit bearing witness with the word yet my heart wanting to fulfill its desire. Part of the struggle was that I didn't have a framework in which to define this intercessory missionary calling, so I found myself somewhat resisting what inwardly I knew to be true.

The next day, I sat in my office thinking about this. I decided to listen to the tape of the prophetic word again. I thought that, outside of that highly subjective moment, I would be able to more objectively consider it. I turned it on and began to listen. When it got to the part about the calling to prayer ministry, the power of the Holy Spirit hit me again and knocked me to the floor. All I could do was say, "Okay, Lord, I don't know what it looks like, but I say, 'Yes.'"

A few years later, I was planting a church. I went out to visit IHOP-KC (I had been out several times before, and my daughter was on staff there), and the Lord powerfully touched my heart regarding its community. I came home and told my wife that I didn't really want to plant a church. I wanted to sit before the Lord as an intercessory missionary at IHOP. It was a good thing because she really didn't want to plant a church at that time either. Six months later, we were living in Kansas City, learning to walk out that calling.

So, a word may point us to something that is not yet fully on our radar, but there is an inner witness that God is in it. The Holy Spirit within us will bear witness with the word. So the two factors in judging a prophetic word are that it bears witness with Scripture and that it bears witness with our own spirit, either inwardly or through circumstances or other words, or both. The key here is the peace of God. Paul expressed this in the following verse:

> Do not be anxious about anything, but in every situation, by prayer and petition, with thanksgiving, present your requests to God. And the peace of God, which transcends all understanding, will guard your hearts and your minds in Christ Jesus (Philippians 4:6-7 NIV).

If there is turmoil, fear, and pressure, then the word might not be from the Lord, or we may be trying to "force-fit" it into circumstances—or perhaps the timing is wrong. We have to trust the peace of God in walking out the promises He has given us.

Determining the Timing

Second, we need to separate out what portion of the word, if any, is for now and what is for later. When I prophesy over someone, there may be two to three aspects of their life that I am addressing. There may be an aspect of the past (promises, experiences), there will be a present aspect touching something in the "now," and there will be things that are yet to come (not necessarily with a specific time frame). The first two aspects are easy to identify, but the third may not seem relevant because it doesn't seem to be applicable at the time. What do we do with these words? We journal them, pray over them, and trust the Lord to fulfill them in His way and in His time.

Recently, a person engaged me in conversation in the coffee shop that is adjacent to the IHOP prayer room. She told me that three years prior I had prophesied something over her. It didn't make sense to her at the time; however, God fulfilled it. I had said that I saw her as a peacemaker, being used by God to bring healing and reconciliation between some ministries. She thought the word odd and felt that, being a lay person and a woman without any authority in her church, it was unlikely such a word could come to pass. A few years later, her church was hosting a conference, and during the conference the issue of reconciling brothers and ministries was highlighted. Her pastor asked her to lead a part of this, and in amazement, there she was, reconciling ministries and ministers. A word given three years earlier was fulfilled in a matter of a couple of hours in a completely unexpected venue, totally set up by God. It's the kindness of God to prepare us ahead of time for situations, both difficult and easy, through a prophetic word given beforehand.

Allowing God to Work out the Word

The third thing one should do when receiving a prophetic word is allow the Lord to unfold it the way He wants to. People often get into trouble by trying to make a word work or come to pass by forcing it into their agendas. We need to set aside agendas.

For example, a young man may receive a prophetic word about receiving the Father's heart and becoming a good father. Perhaps he has had his eye on a young lady and has considered the possibility of marriage. He may take that word and tell the young lady the Lord has spoken to him—that she is supposed to marry him! This has happened so many times, and the result is usually that the other person runs in the opposite direction as fast as she can! Then, the one trying to fit the word into his personal agenda ends up disappointed, wondering why God didn't fulfill His word.

I served in prophetic ministry at IHOP-KC for over nine years. Many of the people to whom I prophesied in the past returned to visit IHOP again. I was often amazed at their stories of how God fulfilled words I had given them, and it usually wasn't in the way they expected it.

One day, twice within an hour, two different ladies approached me with their stories of how He fulfilled His word. I even remembered the words I gave them when they reminded me, and I actually could recall thoughts I had while prophesying to them of how I thought these words might come to pass. I didn't tell them those thoughts because they were my thoughts, and not part of the words the Lord was releasing.

For example, I had prophesied over one lady that the Lord was going to take her on a pilgrimage. He was going to open the doors, supply all the needs, and this would be a great pleasure to her as He showed her His favor. One thought I had, and she confessed she had considered it, was that maybe she would be moving to IHOP! I didn't tell her that (I would never prophesy to a person that they should move to IHOP). She returned home, and within two weeks a friend bought her round-trip tickets to Rome, Italy. She told me she stayed in castles with people of high standing, visited the Vatican, and then returned home after a few weeks, the whole trip costing her nothing. I told her that I would like that word back to use it myself.

Within an hour, a second lady came to me and shared how the Lord fulfilled a prophetic word I had given her. She visited from Hong Kong and had done an IHOP commission (a short-term IHOP program), and I had prophesied three things over her during her stay. First, that she would not lose what she gained at IHOP, but that she would actually use it; that she would do signs and wonders; and that she would pray over the land from the high places. In my own mind, I pictured her with a prayer group going into the mountains and praying over the high places in the land. I didn't say that to her because, again, these were my thoughts of how it might unfold but were not part of what the Lord was saying to her. She told me that she had been used to heal the sick (signs and wonders) and had also grown in the knowledge of God in the things she received at IHOP. But it was the third thing that God fulfilled in a way neither of us would have imagined. She ended up being recruited by an influential woman to be a governmental intercessor. The office where the prayer meetings were held was in the highest building in Hong Kong, and the prayer room was in the highest office in the building, with windows overlooking the entire city. She was praying over Hong Kong, literally, from the highest places in the city.

These two stories, given to me on the same day, within an hour, were like little kisses of encouragement from God regarding the fruitfulness and blessing of prophetic ministry. In both cases, however, I could see that God fulfilled these words in ways we never could have figured out on our own. From these stories, we see how important it is to allow God to work out the details of how a prophetic word is fulfilled. We must not force them into our own agendas. We should pray for the fulfillment of His word, understanding we can't make it come to pass. But if we pray over it occasionally, we will be more likely to see the signs of its coming to pass than we would be if we placed it on the shelf and forgot about it. This is part of how we steward prophetic promises, occasionally lifting them to the Lord in prayer and intercession. We look at our personal prophetic history and pray over the promises that are connected to it.

A friend of mine gave me a prophetic word at an "IHOP One Thing" conference in December of 2005. There were several aspects to it, but the main thing was that she saw me over the San Francisco skyline hearing things and writing them down. I grew up in California and had ministered in San Francisco on a couple of occasions but had no inclination at the time to move there or visit there (she didn't say that I should do either, by the way). It wasn't on my radar at all. It wasn't a word that immediately bore witness and brought a resounding, "Yes, Lord," to my spirit. But because I trusted the vessel, I decided to steward it by praying for San Francisco. I included it in my regular prayer list, asking God to do something in that city. No huge burden, no realm of glory, just simple thirty-second prayers (they do all count, you know).

A few months later, while I was praying for San Francisco, the Lord spoke to me about the city. He told me there was a Goliath over the city that was daring the churches to try anything they wanted; he was threatening to tear it down. Then, the Lord told me He would raise up the young Davids in the city to build the house of prayer and bring down Goliath. He would raise up the intercessors and worship leaders and the young watchmen in the church, and they would bring Goliath down. I thought, *Cool, I have some more ammunition to pray now.*

As a result, my thirty-second prayers became one- or two-minute prayers as I prayed for the raising up of houses of prayer. About four months after that, the Lord spoke to me again about the city. He said that He was going to reverse the curse of Haight/Ashbury. The Haight/Ashbury district was the heart of the hippie movement in the sixties, where the sexual revolution, drugs, and eastern religion hit the West Coast like a freight train. I was famil-iar with this because I was saved out of this movement into the Jesus Movement in 1970. The Lord said He would raise up another youth movement that would be addicted to Jesus and holiness instead of drugs and sex, and He would raise up musicians like the ones who emerged in the sixties, only they would be pure of heart and would lead worship movements. *Great*, I thought, and I added this promise to my prayer arsenal for the city.

I continued to steward this prophetic word in the place of prayer (and I still do to this day). The next year, 2006, rolled around, and I was involved again with prophetic ministry teams at the One Thing conference. After finishing an afternoon prophetic session, I was walking back to the main auditorium when a lady and her daughter stopped me. I had never met them before and hadn't a clue what they wanted. The woman told me her daugh-ter felt strongly impressed I was supposed to pray for her. I asked where they were from, and she told me they were from San Fran-cisco. They were part of a group that was planting houses of prayer in the San Francisco Bay area. My heart exploded inside me! I told them that I had been praying for them for a year and God had some promises for them. They gathered the rest of their team, and we spent time praying and prophesying together. It was exactly a year to the day I had received that prophetic word and decided to steward it in the place of prayer. I walked away laugh-ing and saying, "Lord, You set me up!" I took joy in the lesson He taught me.

We steward our prophetic words by praying for them and keeping them before the Lord. It may be years before some of them fully come to pass, but He is faithful to do what He promises He will do.

MISCELLANEOUS ENCOURAGEMENTS
AND CAUTIONS

Below are some other simple encouragements and guidelines to follow in giving prophetic words.

Be very careful in the giving of words that are highly futuristic and directional. Many people have come to despise prophecy because an overzealous prophesier spoke wonderful and awesome things over them, saying these things would take place in a given time, but their words never came to pass. It might be a good idea to put ourselves in the other guy's shoes and think about how we would feel if we received words full of promises that were supposed to happen in a particular time frame and then didn't. What kind of mental and spiritual traffic could that create? Questions like, "Did I miss it, Lord? Did I do something wrong that prevented the word from happening?" might come to mind.

Sincere believers who totally buy into the words they receive could be brought into a lot of unnecessary stress because we were so sure about the timing. It's much better to err on the side of caution and leave the timing of a word more open-ended. If you feel sure you are right on the timing, then you should also be prepared to be held accountable and to go back and apologize and admit you were wrong if you miss it. If prophesiers held themselves to this standard, they would be less reckless in giving words with imposed time frames! Even when we really feel like we know a timing aspect with a word, we need to be careful to *submit the word more than declare the word, and encourage the person to seek the Lord and not make major decisions based on that word alone.* At the same time, if we are giving words about timing and we are missing it a lot, we need to dial down, back off, and let the Lord teach us a better way.

Encourage people not to be dependent on prophetic words, especially in the major areas of their lives. I have been asked at times to prophesy future decisions or specific directions over people.

One man wanted to know if he should plant a church or take an existing church as a pastor. Another man wanted to know what he should major in at school. Someone else wanted me to prophesy about who his wife would be. People shouldn't confuse prophecy with fortune-telling!

I have personally found, from both giving and receiving words, that God doesn't want me to depend on a prophetic word to make the major decisions of my life. Marriage, vocational changes, geographic moves, and major purchases should not be made on the basis of a single prophetic word. Abba wants to be the One we run to for these decisions. Some would rather take prophetic short-cuts instead of having to wrestle with the Lord for these issues. Whenever they have a crisis or a major decision, they seek out the prophetic vessel for guidance and a word. Jesus reserves the right as our Bridegroom King to be the One who leads in these choices. If my wife came to me one day and told me she sold our house because she had a meeting with a wise realtor who knew the market and suggested it would be a good idea, I would be outraged! Such a decision shouldn't be made outside the marriage relationship with a stranger. So Jesus, as our Bridegroom, reserves the right to be the One who makes those decisions with us.

There were times during ministry transitions that I would have greatly appreciated a good prophetic word to tell me what my next major move should be. I would go to conferences all fired up, asking the Lord to speak to me through a word. I would sit in the front row, right in the path of the prophetic speaker, waiting for ministry time. He would nail the people around me and go by me like I wasn't even there! I said, "Lord, what? Am I invisible?"

To my surprise, He said, "Yes, to everyone but Me."

He wanted me to work it out with Him so I could get His heart on the matter, something I would have missed if I received the word from someone else. Likewise, I have found in many cases that, once I wrestled through the situation with God and made a decision, I would often then receive a prophetic word confirming the decision.

Another important point to remember is that, *as you grow in the prophetic, be careful not to confuse your identity with your gifting.* This doesn't only refer to spiritual gifts; it applies across the board to all we do. There are some who make being prophetic their goal, thinking that, if they can become accomplished and recognized in ministry, they will find fulfillment. The danger in this is it opens the door for disappointment and offense. It seems fine when everyone thinks you are great and your gift is in demand, but if the Lord brings a season where your gift levels out or goes dormant, or someone more gifted comes along and is promoted ahead of you, you can end up offended and frustrated. Often, the Lord Himself will allow such things to happen because He wants our hearts primarily connected to who He is and not what we do. We are His beloved, not because of a gift, but because of the cross. Revelation 21:7 says, "He who overcomes will inherit all things, and I will be his God and he will be My son."

If we invest our identity in what we do above who we are, we will find ourselves often disappointed and tempted to become bitter or offended when we feel slighted, rejected, or overlooked. At the end of the day, we don't stand as ministers or gifted ones; we stand as sons and daughters.

Intimacy falls under the first commandment where we are to know and love God and be loved by Him. *Ministry* falls under the second commandment where we are to love others with the gifts and callings and blessings we have been given, as well as receiving those of others. We are to find our identity in God and let the gifting flow from our relationship to Him.

Your success in the Kingdom doesn't depend on how others view your gifts, talents, or abilities. You are already a success because Abba has set His seal on you. Embracing this will give us great freedom to grow in ministry and, at the same time, increase our appreciation of the gifts and ministries of others.

As you grow in your gift, also be aware of the subtle temptation to use it for manipulation. The prophet Micah rebuked the priests and the prophets for using their ministries for personal gain and selfish ambition (see Mic. 3:11). There are three ways this can happen. First, people can be tempted to use the prophetic to impress other people, thinking others will accept or like them if they give a good word. Second, using the gift to gain favor or goods is also out of bounds. Trying to boost the offering or gain spiritual prominence by speaking a flattering prophetic word is a temptation many have given in to. The third temptation is in trying to influence people's decisions by using the prophetic to do so. I have seen this in both corporate and personal prophecy.

I was told by a pastor there was a woman in his church who would publicly prophesy that God was unhappy with the leadership because they weren't in step with the Spirit. She was trying to use a prophetic platform to air her personal feelings. Even if she did have a word from the Lord, to give it in that way would be completely manipulative. Such a word should be shared in private with leadership so it could be discerned and weighed, not publicly where the spiritually immature could be wrongly influenced and a divisive spirit released. Unless an individual's gift has been recognized and approved by the leadership to prophesy freely in corporate meetings, any corporate word should first be submitted to leaders before releasing it. This is especially true with words containing correctional or directional elements. Even those who have freedom to prophesy should submit their words to leadership before releasing them. Such words should be written out and submitted to leaders for their consideration. This process is discussed in more detail in the last chapter on leadership. For now, I just want to make the point that corporate prophetic words should never be reflections of personal agendas, no matter how much a person may feel he has the "thus saith the Lord." It is still manipulation.

I have heard some heartbreaking stories of how manipulation has functioned in personal prophecy. One woman told me her pastor's wife prophesied over her that negative things would happen to her if she left their church. That is tantamount to witchcraft! When people use the prophetic to build their own crowds or kingdoms, or when they use it to cause people to lean on them and depend on them to be the one who hears from God for them, they are practicing prophetic witchcraft. This is the type of behavior that is found in cults and must be avoided. All of us would say we would never do any of these things, but the enemy can be so subtle. If we are not careful, we may find ourselves doing the very practices we know are wrong. If so, the best thing to do is confess, repent, and move forward. I have a couple of brothers in Christ whom I have asked to immediately confront me if they see me do anything that is even slightly manipulative. We must pursue purity in our motives as we grow in our gifting.

Along these same lines, *don't confuse gifting with character, anointing, or doctrinal correctness.* An accurate prophetic word doesn't mean the prophesier possesses good character or sound doctrine. God doesn't give the gift based on seniority or maturity, but He gives it to the hungry. A new believer may prophesy accurately but not yet be mature in his faith or his doctrine. This may lead to some opinionated viewpoints that slip into his teaching. Don't make the assumption that a good prophetic word means the giver's character, doctrine, or viewpoint is fully matured and developed. Neither does it mean he or she is a false prophet; it just means there is room for growth in the word and in sanctification. Practice the concepts previously mentioned in learning to discern prophetic words.

Don't try to explain how the word will come to pass or counsel people what to do with it. As I shared before, there have been times I have prophesied, and in my mind I have had an idea of how the word might unfold. When this happens, I keep these thoughts to myself, and I am usually glad I did. I have had so many people talk to me a few years after receiving a word, and they were excited about how the Lord fulfilled it. It almost never happens the way I thought it would.

A young man in one of the internships I taught once asked me, "What is the wildest prophecy you ever gave?" My answer was, "All of them are wild. Not so much in the craziness or accuracy of the word given, but rather in the inconceivable ways in which God unfolds them." I have given words that seemed insignificant to me, not weighty at all, only to have the person later tell me how crazy it was in the way it came to pass. Encourage people to pray over the word and leave the unfolding of it to God.

Don't prophesy by natural appearance. I learned a lesson many years ago when I went to a hospital to pray for an older lady in my congregation who was having cancer surgery. As I walked through the lobby, my path crossed that of a young man. He was dressed in black with a long trench coat and black hat. Our eyes met for a moment as we passed each other. I said to myself, *This is one hard young man.* We forget that the Lord is always listening to our thoughts, and He surprised me when He broke in and said, "He's not hard; he's scared."

I said, "Okay, Lord, forgive me for judging wrongly." I continued into the room where my church member was and had some general conversation before praying for her. While we were speaking, this same young man walked into the room and greeted his grandma! He loved her and was afraid of losing her, and that was what the Lord saw.

The Lord corrected Samuel when he went to Jesse's house to anoint a new king. He was about to choose Eliab, the eldest son, based on natural appearance, but the Lord told him that Eliab was not the one and that God judges the heart, not the outward appearance (see 1 Sam. 16:6-7). Trying to prophesy by people's appearance is the same as reading people. And once again, we don't read people.

I recommend you read James a lot. It has great advice regarding our speech, the use of our tongues, and prophesying out of the wisdom from above with godly motives.

Remember to minister in love and humility. Value the dignity of the person you are ministering to. Remember that the gift is not about you; it is about them.

Stay humble and teachable. If you are wrong or make a mistake, don't spiritualize it away or say it means something other than what it is. When we minister in the prophetic, we are taking risks. There will be times we miss it in the interpretation and/or application. If we are to grow in the gift, we must be able to recognize our mistakes and learn from them. We also must be willing to go back and make things right.

I was ministering in a church with some ministry students, and one of them called out a couple and had them stand. He never identified them as husband and wife but simply shared what he was hearing from God for them. I had a little more and began prophesying about their personalities and how they related to one another in their marriage. I began to hear some quiet laughter among the congregation, and the pastor came over with a smile on his face and whispered to me that they weren't married! I acknowledged my mistake to the congregation. They very graciously tried to let me off the hook. One person spoke up that maybe my word was an allegory about the Bride and Jesus. Another person said something else. The truth was, I made an assumption, and it was wrong. I made a mistake, and it was my responsibility to apologize. I excused myself from the platform and took the couple into a side room, where I apologized to them for any embarrassment I caused them and asked them to forgive me. They gladly forgave me. Then, they shared a side story with me.

Apparently, the couple had been engaged to be married, but the young man broke it off because he feared the young lady might make him backslide. He never told her that; he just broke it off without explanation. They both backslid and eventually gave their lives back to God, and this visit to church was sort of a first date. This was the first time the young lady heard the explanation from the young man as to why he broke off the engagement. They told me that other than the part about being married, my word was essentially accurate. I ended up being the mediator as they shared their hearts with one another. About six months later they were married, and I was invited to the wedding.

I tell this story because, afterward, there were some who said that it was a divine mistake, meaning that it was God ordained. I am glad it turned out well, but the point is I really did miss it, and I really needed to make it right. Part of the problem was that in the back of my heart lurked some pride, and when we began the ministry time, I wanted to show off the prophetic gift. I had a dream that night in which I was riding a very fast motorcycle on the freeway. I got off the freeway but was going so fast I could barely stop the bike. This happened twice in the dream. The third time the bike actually went out from under me when I tried to stop because I was going too fast. The Lord spoke to me, reminding me gently but firmly that the prophetic is a powerful gift in the Kingdom and those who will move best in it will be those who walk with a teachable, humble, servant-hearted spirit. We must view our role in the prophetic from the idea that we are to serve. We must be open to accountability, correction, and teaching. By the way, I never prophesy over a couple now without asking first if they are married!

Don't equate delivery style with the anointing. It's not the volume and voice intonations, or lack thereof, that make a prophetic word true or not. It's the Holy Spirit, and He works through a variety of styles and personalities. Don't try to be like the guy you saw at the conference or on TV. Dial down and be yourself.

Don't look for and prophesy people's weaknesses and darkness. We all have our battles to fight. When we receive negative things about people, turn them into positive invitations. If you perceive someone is bound by a sin, ask God what his purpose and destiny is. Communicate God's mercy, love, and calling. Challenge him to pursue holiness (without reference to his sin) so he can fulfill God's purpose in his life.

Don't take on a Messiah complex. As a person grows in prophetic ministry and their words increase in power and accuracy, many in their church may seek them out for a word. It will seem like those seeking them out are always in dire need to hear the word of the Lord for their emergencies. The pull on the prophetic gifting in you can be strong because you so much want to minister and serve people. You may feel like it is your responsibility to have that word that rescues and delivers others in their circumstances. Resist the temptation to take this on. I have had people ask me if they should marry a particular person, accept a particular job, or move to a particular location. We are not fortune-tellers, and it is not for us to take on the responsibility to answer every question or prophesy the fulfillment of everyone's needs. This can shortchange something God wants to teach them, and can lead us into soulish ministry.

Be user-friendly in your choice of words when you prophesy. In the past I encouraged our IHOP teams to avoid the use of IHOP-ese. We used many words and phrases (e.g., forerunner, end-times messenger, dark but lovely, Sermon on the Mount lifestyle) very often within our tribe. But we share a point of reference that others do not. Perhaps there are words and phrases often used within your local setting that would be foreign to a visitor's understanding. Other Christian cultures or churches may use language that is exclusive to their groups, too. We need to speak to people in everyday language they can understand.

Begin where you are. Ask the Lord about the people around you. Who does He want to speak to? There is only one way to grow in prophetic ministry and that is to prophesy! Books and seminars are helpful, but it's only in the practice that your gift will develop. In this light, get feedback from people when you can. After you have prophesied, hold your own personal debrief, asking yourself questions like: "Did I hit the mark? Where could I have done better? How did the threefold process flow? How did most of the revelation come (words, pictures, impressions, etc.)?" Use these times to pray and seek the Lord for the growth of your gift.

Take a long-range perspective. If one of the major expressions of God in your life is the gift of prophecy, then what can you do to steward the gift? Where do you want to be with your gifting in a year? In five years? What steps do you need to take to get there? What are you asking God to do? What do you need to do? Take the gift and its development seriously, and steward it wisely.

Getting Plugged In

1. What are the things in this chapter that have challenged your perception in both giving and receiving prophetic words?

2. Have you started a prophetic journal? If not, begin one. This can be done on your laptop, or it can be handwritten. It should include prophetic words you have received along with impactful dreams, visions, or encounters you have had with God. If you have such a journal, review it and note things that have come to pass, things that may be in the process of happening now, and things not yet fulfilled.

3. As you do the above exercise, are there things that really touch you as you write and review your prophetic history? Take a few moments and lift these promises to the Lord with prayer and thanksgiving.

Section Two

CULTIVATING A PROPHETIC SPIRIT

THE MECHANICS OF PROPHESYING ARE SIMPLE. I REGULARLY teach two-hour seminars where I cover the basic mechanics of how to prophesy and then release people to prophesy. I have watched over and over again as people who have never prophesied before go for it for the very first time and do it well. There are always ways to improve and grow in our gifting, but at the end of the day it's not rocket science. The principles aren't that difficult to understand.

Proverbs tells us that the eye that sees and the ear that hears, "the Lord has made them both" (20:12). He created us to see and hear, both in the natural and the spirit. In *The Way of the Mystics*, the foundations of Christian mysticism are based on three principles—God exists, God is personal, and God desires a personal communion with each and every one of us.[1] These principles are also foundational to prophetic ministry. If we can be quiet and listen, or pay attention and watch, we can see, hear, and prophesy. As Paul tells us, all may prophesy (see 1 Cor. 14:31). This is the easy part.

There are two questions we need to ask ourselves if we want to see mature prophetic ministry continue to grow in our lives. One is, "How deep, mature, and lasting will my prophetic ministry be?"

The other is, "How do I cultivate a prophetic spirit?" The answers to these questions are found in the pursuit of friendship and intimacy with Christ. A prophetic vessel is like an iceberg. In ministry, only the top 10 percent shows on the surface, while the 90 percent when we prophesy, but God looks at the whole iceberg, as it were. He wants us to go beyond clear and accurate words. He wants our hearts and lives to be deeply rooted in Him. He wants our character to begin to line up with the anointing He wants to release in and through us. He loves to give us gifts, but He also wants us to grow up in our character to match the gifts He releases.

To me, a person with a prophetic spirit is simply defined as the one who has cultivated a life that is rich in the place of prayer and the Word of God. Prophecy and every other gift and calling we express are birthed in and rooted in our identity in God. Spending time with God in the secret place must become one the most important things in our lives. The cry of our hearts is the same as David's—that the reward of our lives would be to gaze on His beauty all our days (see Ps. 27:4).

Cultivating a prophetic spirit isn't done with the purpose of being more prophetic, but rather with the purpose of attaining a spirit of wisdom and revelation so that we might know Jesus better (see Eph. 1:15-17). If we are moving forward in this goal, becoming stronger in the prophetic will be the natural outgrowth and result.

Many people see a prophetic minister in a church or conference setting and become enamored with the ministry and begin to pursue and covet that type of ministry. In truth, most people will never minister in the same platform context they see that prophetic vessel minister in. It doesn't mean their ministry won't be just as effective in their context and circle of influence. The measure of success in prophetic ministry, as with any other ministry, isn't the number of people who come to the seminars, or even how accurate the word is, though that is important. The measure of success is how obedient we are with what God has given us in the context He has set us in. The foundation of that success will be determined by how deep we go in the knowledge of God and, conversely, how much of us He possesses. These factors are all part of the journey of intimacy with God.

There is another quote from *The Way of the Mystics* that is very applicable here. It is attributed to Bernard of Clairvaux:

> It would be best, he said, if people resembled reservoirs, opening their souls to be filled with God's Spirit, then allowing the overflow to empower their ministry to others. But instead, too many people resemble canals. The water of the Holy Spirit flows through their lives but it disappears as soon as it arrives. "They want to pour it forth before they have been filled," he writes. "They are more ready to speak than to listen, impatient to teach what they have not grasped, and full of presumption to govern others while they know not how to govern themselves."[2]

Intimacy with God is foundational to the life of every believer, not only in terms of prophetic ministry, but in every aspect of our lives in God. The more mature the tree, the better the fruit tastes. Ministry impact deepens when the branches are more deeply rooted in the vine (see John 15:5). This goes to the root of my security in God and my confidence before Him. It's hard to trust someone you barely know. It's hard to operate in confidence when you only have knowledge about a subject but no experience in that subject. When we prophesy, we are speaking for Him; thus it should be the desire of our hearts to be ever increasing in both the knowledge and experience of His love.

Many believers have a lot of knowledge about God but not a lot of experience in God. When it comes to stepping up or stepping out in God, their confidence level isn't steady. If they have had a good week, if they read their Bible a little and prayed a little and didn't sin too much or blow it too badly, then their confidence level is above average. If they had a bad week, prayed or read very little, yelled at their kids, and watched things they shouldn't have, their confidence level is low. In other words, their confidence is more in who they are and how they have behaved than it is in who God is and how He feels or what He says about them. If we feel badly about ourselves, we have very little confidence to prophesy for God. God wants us to have intimate knowledge of Him, and He has given us His Word and His Spirit to lead us into the vastness of His love and knowledge through the experience of personal relationship.

There are several biblical pictures that demonstrate this, but two stand out. They are the *Father's Heart* and the *Bridal Paradigm*. God created man to enjoy and be enjoyed by Him, and to make him a partner in His purposes in the earth. The wonder of the revelation of the Father's heart is that He turns prodigals into sons and daughters, transforms beggars into princes, sets them in His family, and ordains them to rule and reign with Him. It's the revelation of unconditional love and unlimited destiny.

The Bridal Paradigm, similarly, is about a peasant girl (that would be us) who becomes betrothed to a King. The first wonder is that the King of the land would set His eyes on a peasant girl and declare her to be absolutely beautiful. The second great wonder is that as she revels in this love, He is transforming her into a queen who will partner with Him in the fulfillment of His testimony. I want to take a deeper look at both of these concepts, and then cover some practical ways of growing in intimacy with this God of wonder who speaks to humans and commands them to prophesy!

NOTES

1.   John Michael Talbot and Steve Rabey, *The Way of the Mystics* (San Francisco: Jossey-Bass, 2006) 7.

2.   Ibid., 39.

Chapter Four

THE FATHER'S HEART 101

I HAVE A DEEP LONGING TO KNOW, SEE, AND LIVE MORE FULLY IN the Kingdom of God. In my pursuit of this goal, I have had encounters with God where He has given me revelation in ways that have caused my heart to soar and my spirit to burn with fiery love for Him. Of all the encounters and revelations I have had with God, there is one that stands out above them all, and it is the simple revelation that the Father loves me, enjoys me, and takes pleasure in me all the time. It's the revelation that Jesus is a lover who is after my heart. He is a glad worker in transforming me into a lover of Him.

Knowing that God takes pleasure in me makes me confident and glad at heart. I am confident before Him in the place of intimate fellowship, and I am confident before Him in the place of ardent intercession. I am confident before Him in praying for the sick, and I am confident before Him in prophesying. I am confident before Him when I have had a phenomenal week, and I am confident before Him when I have sinned and made a big mess of things (provided I am walking in repentance and forgiveness).

I have come to know that I am His favorite (smile). He not only loves me, but He actually likes me, and 24/7 my face is beautiful to Him and my voice sweet. Such revelation comes to me daily as I pray His Word and fellowship with the Holy Spirit who lives in me. The truth is, beloved, He's crazy about you, too. All of His children are His favorites!

This concept of the pleasure of God over us is rooted deeply in Scripture, and God desires it to be real in our experience. The pictures of the Father's Heart and the Bridal Paradigm are expressions of this concept. If we are to prophesy from the Father's heart and out of the Bridegroom's mouth, it's vital for us to grow in understanding the heart of God over the nations and over people.

The Importance of Knowing the Father's Heart

I have prayed for many people, both young and old—men and women—to come into the knowledge of the truth that they are loved by Abba God. The message and experience many have picked up from church, home, or peers is that the Father is not happy with them and that they need to do more, try harder, and be better if they are ever to expect anything from Him. If we are ever going to be the Malachi generation that turns the hearts of the fathers to the children and the hearts of the children to the fathers, we are going to need to understand this (see Mal. 4:6). The fact is, multitudes of people see God as an angry or disappointed Father who is never satisfied with the performance or offerings of their lives.

However, the truth is that He is mostly a glad God of mercy, releasing judgment only for a moment when long expressed mercy has run its course and been rejected. Even when His judgments are required in our lives, they are only released to the measure we need to bring us back to His mercy because He loves us too much to leave us in our sin.

Beginning with his first appearance in the garden, the enemy has done his best to portray God as a Father who is holding out on His children, stoically enforcing harsh rules and demanding perfection while arbitrarily and randomly doling out pain and judgment. This is the view that many believers live under today. They think God is a Father who can never be fully satisfied, that He is always going to require a little more than we are able to give. Add to this the demonic attack on the place of fathers in our culture, and the picture only gets worse. The emphasis on materialism, success in the marketplace, and personal fulfillment has led many fathers to become preoccupied with their own lives and successes at the expense of relationship with their children. This isn't limited to the world. These same characteristics are often found in the church and ministry as well.

Additionally, often the negative experiences of fathers get passed down to the children in terms of not communicating and expressing value, positive affirmation, and love in an unconditional manner. Every generation carries its own expression of brokenness into family life, and even the very best parents still have their flaws. I often joke with my children that they should be thankful for the ministries of inner healing because something I do at some point in their lives will probably wound them, but inner healing is available to help heal their wounds!

When people experience brokenness in their lives, it can make it difficult for them to relate to a Father who loves them unconditionally. They may know it in their heads and have a right theology, but they don't know it in confidence in their hearts. This is the experience of a great many people in the body of Christ, and it's robbing them of the confidence to joyfully be who they are in God.

Three predominant views I run into are that God is absent, distant, and uncaring; that He is harsh, angry, and judgmental; or that He is unpredictable, allowing pain to touch our lives but doing little to alleviate it. Such views foster an unhealthy way to relate to Him as a Father. Our experience changes, however, when we recognize the lies we have believed about Him, come into agreement with the truth of who He is, and let that transfer into our hearts through the means of invitation and fellowship with the Holy Spirit. In this process we learn that He is not absent, distant, and uncaring.

Consider what the prophet Zephaniah said about Jehovah.

> *Sing, O daughter of Zion! Shout, O Israel! Be glad and rejoice with all your heart, O daughter of Jerusalem! The Lord has taken away your judgments, He has cast out your enemy. The King of Israel, the Lord, is in your midst; you shall see disaster no more. In that day it shall be said to Jerusalem: "Do not fear; Zion, let not your hands be weak. The Lord your God in your midst, the Mighty One, will save; He will rejoice over you with gladness. He will quiet you with His love. He will rejoice over you with singing" (Zephaniah 3:14-17).*

We see in this portion of Scripture Abba Father who is near, who fights for us, who cuts off the judgments of the enemy against us, and who sings over us with joy. He is not distant and uncaring. He is not a detached observer, watching us struggle on our own. He is taking our case, fighting for us, and victoriously singing over us.

I was praying for people after a church service, and I asked a young lady how I could pray for her. She answered in a somewhat demanding way, "I want God to show me where He was when I was hurting." She wasn't looking for a pat theological answer. She was looking for the Father who is supposed to be near.

I simply said, "Why don't we ask Him?"

She asked Him and barely got the words out before she began to weep. Over the next fifteen minutes, she was locked in with Abba.

I had a few helpful words of knowledge, which I simply prayed over her in four or five sentences. She was meeting with Abba, and He was answering her question. After a while, she stood up, face glowing. I asked her what had happened, and she told me the Lord met her in her pain and showed her His perspective. Turns out that her mother had been under pressure to abort her, but resisted, choosing to give birth. In the process of her birth, her mother died. She had been carrying guilt toward herself and anger at God ever since.

In her encounter with the Lord, He showed her that He was there, that she was beautiful, that her mother's death was not her fault, and that she should honor the sacrifice her mother made so she could live. He fulfilled Zephaniah's prophecy on a personal level and in a matter of minutes. He quieted her heart with His love and released His song of rejoicing over her life. He cut off the accusations of the enemy and stood in her midst.

God is not distant, but He is near. This is the Father who wants to bring us into His heart and have us prophesy from that perspective. He is anything but stoic and harsh. James tells us His "mercy triumphs over judgment" (James 2:13). He's not looking for reasons to punish us when we break the slightest commandment. Psalm 139 tells us He is the opposite.

For You formed my inward parts; You covered me in my mother's womb. I will praise You, for I am fearfully and wonderfully made; marvelous are Your works, and that my soul knows very well. My frame was not hidden from You, when I was made in secret, and skillfully wrought in the lowest parts of the earth. Your eyes saw my substance, being yet unformed. And in Your book they all were written, the days fashioned for me, when as yet there were none of them. How precious also are Your thoughts to me, O God! How great is the sum of them! If I should count them they would be more in number than the sand; when I awake, I am still with You (Psalm 139:13-18).

The whole of the Psalm is a declaration of His nearness, affection, and tender mercies toward us, but the above verses really give insight to the preciousness and value of every human life to Him. He loved us before the foundations of the earth and was there even at our conception. He smiled over every aspect of our bodies, and He called us beautiful. Furthermore, we are always on His mind. His thoughts toward us outnumber the sands of the sea, and they aren't condemning or accusing. They are good continually, for a hope and a future (see Ps. 34; 139; Jer. 33; Rom. 8).

I prayed for a young man once who was of a particular ethnic background. He attended a school where he was a minority and was constantly teased over his physical features and was bullied and mocked much of his life. He also experienced a lot of strife at home, and his father at times told him he was a worthless troublemaker. He grew up angry at his dad, angry at God, and hating himself and his culture for how he looked. He couldn't fathom that God could actually like him and could even be proud of him as a son.

We prayed through Psalm 139, renouncing the lies of the enemy, coming into agreement with who God said he was and what God as a Father thought about him. (Incidentally, when we pray Scripture over our lives, we are actually prophesying over our hearts.) Then, we asked the Father to reveal and release His love into his heart. This young man's life was transformed as he was set free from self-hatred and received the affection of Abba. He experienced the freedom of the sons of God as he understood that the Father had a future for him and it was good. This is the heart of the Father who feels the brokenness of people and is raising up a prophetic generation to prophesy to the broken and lost that there is a fountain of healing open to them.

Lastly, God is not cruel and unpredictable. Jesus's best friend John had a powerful revelation of the Father's love, and he passed it on to us in his letters. He described the Father's heart toward us in the following way:

> See what great love the Father has lavished on us, that we should be called children of God! And that is what we are! The reason the world does not know us is that it did not know him. Dear friends, now we are children of God, and what we will be has not yet been made known. But we know that when Christ appears, we shall be like him, for we shall see him as he is (1 John 3:1-2 NIV).

I prayed for another young man at a conference who grew up with a father who defined manhood by carousing in bars, womanizing, fighting, and not taking anything from anyone. He continually impressed upon his son that, if he wasn't tough, then he wasn't a man. Toughness was defined by not crying, jumping into fights, and holding his liquor. Weakness or sensitivity of heart was cause for ridicule. He didn't know what to expect from his dad from one moment to the next—a hug or a hit.

This young man had become a father, and he wanted to represent Abba rightly to his own child. As we prayed, Abba released several words of knowledge regarding old pictures, phrases, and curses spoken over him. The young man wept as heavenly Father not only healed his heart, but changed his paradigm of fatherhood, assuring him that he would be a good father to his son.

I cannot say this enough. Abba is not unpredictable and cruel. He is love. And He is willing to reveal that love and affection into our hearts in mercy, grace, and healing. David said that as an earthly father shows pity to his children, so our heavenly Father delights to show us mercy. He said, "For He knows our frame; He remembers that we are dust" (Ps. 103:14).

God's anger is but for a moment, but His mercy endures forever (see Ps. 30:5). In fact, in Psalm 59 David refers to God as his God of mercy. He said, "I will wait for You, O You his Strength; for God is my defense. My God of mercy shall come to meet me; God shall let me see my desire on my enemies" (Ps. 59:9-10).

This is the same picture Jesus so beautifully painted in the story of the prodigal son (see Luke 15:11-31). The father saw his broken and penitent boy when he was yet at some distance, and he went running to him, greeting him with an embrace while calling his servant to bring new clothes and to prepare the fatted calf for a celebration. The son had come to grips with the reality of his sin and how he had grieved his loving father. His remorse, sense of failure, and lack of self-worth were so deep that he would have been glad to live on his dad's property in the house with the servants. His father, however, would not entertain such an idea. Sons don't belong in the servants' quarters; they belong in their father's house. He re-blessed him, re-dressed him, celebrated his future, and brought him into his house.

We have all been prodigals. We have all been adopted into the Father's love. Jesus Himself had much to say about the Father, how He sees us, and how we are to relate to Him. Philip, one of His disciples, asked Jesus to show him the Father. Jesus responded, "Have I been with you so long, and yet you have not known Me, Philip? He who has seen Me has seen the Father; so how can you say, 'Show us the Father'?" (John 14:9).

In other words, the same heart Jesus demonstrated in healing, forgiving, and restoring was in the heart of the Father. In fact, Jesus said that He only did what He saw the Father do. All Jesus's ministry and motives were rooted in the heart of the Father. The most significant expression of this came through Jesus's answer to the disciples' request to teach them how to pray. The first thing

Jesus taught them was totally foundational to the rest of the prayer. He said, "In this manner, therefore, pray: Our Father in heaven, hallowed be Your name. Your kingdom come. Your will be done on earth as it is in heaven" (Matt. 6:9-10).

The first thing Jesus taught about prayer is that—in the heart of the Almighty God who rules and reigns over every universe, who is High and Holy and dwells in the Holy place—He has the heart of a Father and has longed to fellowship with us before the foundations of the earth. He is a benevolent Father who loves us as His children. Through Jesus, we come before a Father who invites us to a throne of grace and longs for us to come near Him in our times of need. Hebrews 4:16 tells us, "Let us therefore come boldly to the throne of grace, that we may obtain mercy and find grace to help in time of need."

The rest of the Lord's Prayer spins off of this foundational truth that God is a Father who loves to fellowship with us. As a Father, He wants to give us our daily bread, forgive our sins, deliver us from the evil one, and partner with us in bringing His Kingdom to the earth. This is the Father who desires us and adopts us into His household. We will still have our wars, our ups and downs, our failures and our successes. None of these things, good or bad, qualify us or disqualify us to come to the Father's table in His house. The blood of His Son has made a way for us, and it's more than theology. He desires for all His sons and daughters to experience the sense of acceptance, love, affection, and destiny He has for us.

I can't separate my prophetic ministry from my daily experience of pursuing and loving Abba. My pursuit and my prophetic ministry aren't two separate things. My confidence and maturity in the latter is the result of my emphasis on the first thing, the One Thing. Because I am loved and accepted as a son, I have confidence to be about my Father's business in all circumstances and situations, not because I have been good enough, but because He is good and I am loved overwhelmingly. Out of this intimate relationship with my Father, I have confidence and freedom to run in the prophetic assignment He has given me in this age. This has been a great help in prophesying over others because it helps me see them through His heart.

GETTING PLUGGED IN

1. Take some time to list all the Scripture references in the above chapter and slowly read through them. Then say them as prayers, allowing the Holy Spirit to encourage and minister to your heart the revelation of how Abba feels about you.

2. As you do the above exercise, ask the Holy Spirit to reveal to you any lie you have come to believe about the Father's heart and feelings for you. Confess it to Him and break your agreement with it in Jesus's name. Then, confess the truths of the scriptures you have read, intentionally coming into agreement with their revelation of who you are before God. Ask Him to heal any broken areas of your heart and to encounter your heart with His deep affections for you.

3. What effect will our view of the Fatherhood of God have on our prophetic ministry?

4. Prophetic words bring both the expression of God's word to people and the expression of God's nature to people. Agree or disagree? Why?

Chapter Five

THE BRIDAL PARADIGM

THE CONCEPT OF THE BRIDAL PARADIGM MAY BE NEW TO MANY, but it's as much rooted in Scripture as is the concept of the Father's heart. The Bridal Paradigm refers to the intimacy and partnership that Jesus desires to have with the Church as His Bride, both now and in the age to come.

In the Garden of Eden, we see the beginnings of the picture of the Bridal Paradigm. After God created man, He noted that it wasn't good for the man to be alone and decided to make for him a wife. He put him to sleep, reached into his side, took out a rib, and made a bride for this son He called *Adam*. Throughout the OT, the promise of a Messiah who would suffer for the sins of humankind pointed to the cross, where similarly the Father, mystically speaking, reached into the side of His Son and pulled out a Bride for Him.

Eve's job was to partner with Adam in their assignment to populate and rule the earth. We know that they blew their assignment and were forced out of the garden. Eve was deceived into eating the forbidden fruit, but Adam was not. He made his decision, not under the deceptive, seductive temptation that Eve did, but with clear and sober understanding of what this act would cost him. In the final analysis, he chose to sacrifice his relationship with his heavenly Father because he would rather live outside the garden with Eve than inside the garden without her. Jesus would do the opposite in another garden later. He would pay the ultimate price to bring the Bride back into the garden!

Throughout the OT, the prophets used bridal language to describe the relationship between God and His people, Israel. When she went astray and worshiped false gods, the prophets often described her as an unfaithful bride who left the husband of her youth. Jeremiah prophesied, for example:

> *The word of the Lord came to me, saying, "Go and cry in the hearing of Jerusalem, saying, 'Thus says the Lord: "I remember you, the kindness of your youth, the love of your betrothal, when you went after Me in the wilderness, in a land not sown. Israel was holiness to the Lord, the firstfruits of His increase. All that devour him will offend; disaster will come upon them," says the Lord'"* (Jeremiah 2:1-3).

God reminds His people of their early love and the marriage covenant they had with Him. He further says, "Can a virgin forget her ornaments, or a bride her attire? Yet My people have forgotten Me days without number" (Jer. 2:32).

Israel was called, as the Bride of the Holy One, to be the beneficiary of His blessings and the nation that would release His blessings and manifest His glory among the nations. Instead, more often than not, she suffered an identity crisis wherein she became more like the nations around her than the Bride of the Holy One. So God would again send prophets to call her back to her marriage covenant with Him. He would say, "Return, O backsliding children...for I am married to you. I will take you, one from a city and two from a family, and I will bring you to Zion" (Jer. 3:14).

The most radical expression is seen in Hosea, where God called the prophet to marry a prostitute as a picture of the way His Bride treated Him. He speaks of the way He will discipline her, to draw her back to Himself.

> *She will chase her lovers, but not overtake them; yes, she will seek them, but not find them. Then she will say, "I will go and return to my first husband, for then it was better for me than now." For she did not know that I gave her grain, new wine, and oil, and multiplied her silver and gold—which they prepared for Baal. ...Therefore, behold, I will allure her, will bring her into the wilderness, and speak comfort to her. I will give her vineyards from there, and the Valley of Achor as a door of hope; she shall sing there, as in the days of her youth, as in the day when she came up from the land of Egypt. And it shall be, in that day...that you will call Me "My Husband," and no longer call Me "My Master," for I will take from her mouth the names of the Baals* (Hosea 2:7-8;14-17).

Much of the prophetic language in verses like the ones above speaks of a day of restoration, when Jesus returns to the earth as King and Israel recognizes Him and receives Him as her Bridegroom King. There are other prophets who spoke similarly. We read:

> *Do not fear, for you will not be ashamed; neither be disgraced, for you will not be put to shame; for you will forget the shame of your youth, and will not remember the reproach of your widowhood anymore. For your Maker is your husband, the Lord of hosts is His name; and your Redeemer is the Holy One of Israel; He is called*

the God of the whole earth. For the Lord has called
you like a woman forsaken and grieved in spirit, like
a youthful wife when you were refused (Isaiah 54:4-6).

King David had revelation of this Bridegroom King, and he
records it in Psalm 45.

You are fairer than the sons of men; grace is poured
upon Your lips; therefore God has blessed You forever.
Gird Your sword upon Your thigh, O Mighty One, with
Your glory and Your majesty. And in Your majesty ride
prosperously because of truth, humility, and righteous-
ness; and Your right hand shall teach You awesome
things. Your arrows are sharp in the heart of the King's
enemies; the peoples fall under You. Your throne, O
God, is forever and ever; a scepter of righteousness is
the scepter of Your kingdom. You love righteousness and
hate wickedness; therefore God, Your God, has anointed
You with the oil of gladness more than Your compan-
ions. ...Listen, O daughter, consider and incline your
ear; forget your own people also, and your father's house.
So the King will greatly desire your beauty; because He
is your Lord, worship Him (Psalm 45:2-7,10-11).

David describes the righteous Messiah as the One who will
conquer the nations and who is the righteous Bridegroom who
calls the Bride into intimacy and partnership. There will be a
day when Israel will recognize Jesus as her Bridegroom King and
will embrace Him even as the Church is called to do now. Part of
the prophetic call of the Church is to provoke Israel to jealousy
through her intimacy and power in Christ and her ardent love and
intercession for Israel.

The essence of the bridal call goes to two things—intimacy and
partnership. Jesus desires you! He values you so deeply and wants
you to know and live in intimacy with Him. He wants all your gifts

and callings to flow out of that place in love and confidence. It's He who picked up the bridal theme in the Gospels. He took it beyond just an application to Israel and actually included the Gentiles. In John 3:16, He included the world as part of His called ones. Jesus referred to other sheep He would have of a different fold, and He prayed to the Father for all who would believe in Him through the preached word of the disciples.

> *And other sheep I have which are not of this fold; them also I must bring, and they will hear My voice; and there will be one flock and one shepherd* (John 10:16).

> *I do not pray for these alone, but also for those who will believe in Me through their word; that they all may be one, as You, Father, are in Me, and I in You; that they also may be one in Us, that the world may believe that You sent Me* (John 17:20-21).

Israel was often referred to as the Bride of the Holy One in the OT. Now, the Holy One who took on human flesh continued the theme, applying it to Himself as the Bridegroom and those who would follow as His Bride. When questioned by the Pharisees and John's disciples as to why they fasted regularly but His disciples did not, Jesus replied:

> *Can the friends of the bridegroom mourn as long as the bridegroom is with them? But the days will come when the bridegroom will be taken away from them, and then they will fast* (Matthew 9:15).

Jesus introduces here a picture of Himself as a Bridegroom and His disciples as friends of the Bridegroom. The interesting thing here is that we all are called to live in a dual capacity. As His Bride, we are to live in intimate fellowship with Him. As friends of the Bridegroom, we are called to serve Him both by partnering with Him in fulfilling our gifts and assignments, but also, in that context, to prepare the Bride to receive her Bridegroom when He returns for her.

So, part of the function of the prophetic gift is to encourage and equip the Bride to walk in the fullness of the knowledge of who Jesus is. God is raising up prophetic friends who will hear and speak what is on His heart for His Bride in every time and season. It's important for us to be walking with Him so we can be listening to the voice of the Bridegroom.

In the parable of the ten virgins in Matthew 25, Jesus spoke of Himself as a coming Bridegroom. Who were the ones who were ready at His coming? They were the five who had stored up the oil of intimacy, making friendship with Him the goal of their lives. This role of friendship with the Bridegroom is the context in which John the Baptist trained his disciples to view Jesus and his role in relation to Him. John 3:27-36 describes John's response to the concern of his disciples over his waning following as compared to Jesus and all the crowds that began to follow Him. He made it clear to them that his ministry was never about himself but was always about Jesus the Bridegroom.

> John answered and said, "A man can receive nothing unless it has been given to him from heaven. You yourselves bear me witness, that I said, 'I am not the Christ,' but, 'I have been sent before Him.' He who has the bride is the bridegroom; but the friend of the bridegroom, who stands and hears him, rejoices greatly because of the bridegroom's voice. Therefore this joy of mine is fulfilled. He must increase, but I must decrease" (John 3:27-30).

John identified himself as the friend of the Bridegroom whose job it was to prepare the Bride to hear Him. It was never about how awesome or big his ministry was. It was always about getting the crowds to prepare their hearts for the coming of the Lamb slain from the foundations of the earth. As His friend, he delighted in His presence. As a servant, he rejoiced to do the work that turned the Bride to the heart of the Bridegroom. The job of the prophetic servant is like John—to stand, hear, and declare the will and voice of the Bridegroom to the Bride.

A key biblical book in this regard is Song of Solomon. It's one of the primary expressions of the Bridal Paradigm in the Scriptures. Writers through the ages have commented on this particular book from many different viewpoints. My purpose is to briefly touch on four highlights in the journey of the Bride that demonstrate Christ's desire for intimate relationship and partnership with His Bride in accomplishing His purposes in the earth. The main point is that His desire is for our works for Him to come out of our intimacy with Him. The Bride is to find her identity in who she is and in whose she is, not in what she does or by her performance. My purpose here is to encourage you to go deeper into the foundation of Christ's affections over you and to challenge you to take your place in the testimony of Jesus, our beloved Bridegroom and King.

The story line of the Song of Solomon is simple. The King has fallen in love with the young Shulamite girl, much to her surprise. The book tracks her journey through the joys and struggles of embracing first love to the maturity of sacrificial love where she learns to follow Him even when the cost involves her comfort and convenience. In this process, she learns not only to love Him, but also to love what He loves as her heart is being prepared to partner with Him as His queen. The story ends with her coming into full maturity, functioning in deep intimacy and affection with Him and in great power on His behalf. In this position, she is willing to stand with Him at the end of the age, loving not her own life even unto death.

STAGE ONE: CONFIDENT LOVE

The Bride's journey begins with her heart being awakened by the love of the King. His affections have overwhelmed her. As her heart is awakened by His tender kindness toward her, she finds herself more and more fascinated in His love. She says:

> Let him kiss me with the kisses of his mouth—for your love is better than wine. Because of the fragrance of your good ointments, your name is ointment poured forth.... Draw me away! ...The king has brought me into his chambers (Song of Solomon 1:2-4).

For our purposes, this would be better translated, "Let him kiss me with the kisses of His Word." Jesus isn't going to kiss us on the mouth (I can hear a collective sigh of relief from the men reading this book!). In this place, she experiences four symbolic expressions of intimacy.

The first is the *kiss of His Word*, which represents the breaking in of the revelation of the depths of Christ's love for us. We come under the influence of the Spirit and the Word together, and it's as if everything we are reading was written just for us. His kiss is the revelation to our hearts that the uncreated Creator, the Resurrected Bridegroom King, has chosen us and pours His affection on our hearts. It's the awakening of a heart to the power of divine grace. He actually desires us. We move Him with a simple, "I love You." He is jealous over us and fights for us. This is the affection of Jesus over the Bride.

The second expression of intimacy she feels is *lovesickness*, as she cries out that His love is better than wine. This is more than the giddiness of infatuation. This touch produces longing in the heart of the Bride. It releases the Psalm 84:2 desire that causes our flesh to cry out for Him and our soul to faint for Him. It's an inner joy that produces an inner hunger for more. He is all she can think about, and when she thinks about Him, she is inebriated with the oil of gladness. To be in His presence is better than the best of wines.

The third expression is *the fragrance of His nearness*. I have five children and have watched them all go through the stages of trying out perfume and aftershave. You know they have overdone it when the fragrance arrives before they do! The most excellent perfumes are made to catch you with just the slightest aroma. They catch your attention and invite you to discover their source.

My wife has exquisite taste in perfume. When I get close to her, I can pick up the scent. The closer I get, the stronger it becomes until I actually carry a little of the fragrance myself. The Bride here has gotten close enough to the Bridegroom that, when He leaves, His fragrance lingers around her.

There is a fragrance of life that comes from Jesus. There is a fragrance of His presence that comes from being near Him. It elevates us, lifts us, and fills us with life. The Bride here has been lifted above the natural realm of this world's fragrance and into a realm that overwhelms her senses with life and love. She wants to carry His fragrance with her wherever she goes.

The last expression of intimacy here is the constant cry of the Bride to come nearer and the reply of the Bridegroom to oblige. "How much of Me do you want?" He asks.

Her cry is, "Draw me away."

His response is to bring her into His chambers.

All these expressions simply describe a heart that has been ruined by love. The King of Glory has captured the heart of this Bride. How can life be the same again? How can she go back to business as usual? This wasn't just a nice date where her heart was moved for a moment. This was an overwhelming, a kidnapping, a full capture of her entire being, and she could never be happy with anything less than this King. He became her magnificent obsession, her source of life, love, and grace.

Unfortunately, this bliss was interrupted by accusations and criticisms, first from without and then from within. We read in verse six of chapter one, "My mother's sons were angry with me." She hadn't been working in her brothers vineyards, and so was accused of being unproductive. This is the voice of those who would say that love is not enough, we must add something of our own goodness to deserve the love of the King. After all, she is young and weak and immature. How could this King love her in this state? Surely something more than simple love must be required. These accusations came to shake her confidence in the love of the Beloved.

She found that these accusations brought forth her own insecurities and doubts, as she says, "My own vineyard I have not kept" (Song of Sol. 1:6). As she is accused by others, she begins to doubt in herself. "Who am I really, that a King could fall in love with me? I have so many weaknesses and faults. I am far from queenly material. I'm kidding myself. This is all too good to be true. How can He love me when I am so dark?" That is the question that goes to the heart of her confidence in being loved by and received by such a wonderful King. He is great; she is unknown. He is powerful; she is weak. He is confident; she seems to waver so often.

In this place, the King comes to reassure her. He is not blind. He can't be deceived by appearance. He knows the condition of the Bride He has chosen, and she is completely lovely to Him. He has set His gaze on her, not to find fault and condemn, but because He enjoys watching the movements of her heart. "Behold, he stands behind our wall; he is looking through the windows, gazing through the lattice" (Song of Sol. 2:9). His assurance to her is, "Yes, I know you are dark and you feel weak. I know you can think of a thousand accusations that declare you are unworthy of My love. So I want to tell you—to Me, You are lovely." The King is assuring and establishing the Bride in the identity of His love. It is true, real, and everlasting. His love isn't surprised or deterred by her weakness.

Jesus is telling us here that we are totally worth the investment He made in us on the cross. You were worth every drop of blood He shed. He has eternal plans for you, because to Him, you are altogether lovely, even in your weakness. He enjoys You. He is gazing into the windows of your soul, and you have captured His heart with your little *yeses* and your acts of love toward Him.

The Bride is becoming steady in love. She has confidence in His unshakeable commitment to her, despite her weakness. This assurance causes her to love Him even more. Now she is able to say, "I am dark, but lovely, O daughters of Jerusalem, like the tents of Kedar, like the curtains of Solomon" (Song of Sol. 1:5).

This is the love that draws us into holiness. Because we are so greatly loved, our desire is to please Him and walk in a manner worthy of His love. It's important for prophetic people to understand this. It isn't our gifting that attracts Jesus to us. It isn't our talent that He defines us by. Our gifting and calling aren't rewards for stepping out in the prophetic; they are the gifts and expressions of His perfect love for us. They aren't based on how good and confident we are, but rather on how good He is.

Our identity isn't in our gifts and what we do. It's in our position, which is based on who we are before Him. When we get this, it frees us to prophesy in any and all circumstances without the pressure of having to prove ourselves or hold back because we aren't sure if He likes us today. His gifts, like His love, aren't dependent on our circumstances, but rather on His goodness and call on our lives. The essence of this identity in love is expressed in Song of Solomon 2:14, "O my dove, in the clefts of the rock, in the secret places of the cliffs, let me see your face, let me hear your voice; for your voice is sweet, and your face is lovely."

The secret place of the cliff represents His wounds, that place where He was pierced with that soldier's spear. He has hidden His Bride in that place, and through His eyes of fiery love He declares to her, "Let me see your face. Let me hear your voice."

Her identity is in Him. He doesn't define her by her strengths or her weaknesses. He defines her by her relationship to Him as His Bride. This causes her heart to be steady in love. To Him, her face is beautiful and her voice sweet 24/7. She can move in His gifts and power based on that foundation of confident love. If you want to know what He thinks of you 24/7, it's revealed in that verse. He loves to see your face and hear your voice, always and forever.

STAGE TWO: SACRIFICIAL LOVE

The second stage of the story is the call of the Bride from the place of first love into the place of sacrificial love. She has known His incredible strengthening, freeing, and intimate love in a place of relative comfort. He has kissed her heart with His encouragement, calmed her fears, and established her in His affection. She would be happy if this was all there were to the story. It would be fine with her if all He did was tell her she was loved, continually feeding her at the banqueting table with wine and raisin cakes. He has something else in mind though. He has destined her for greatness. Yes, He will continue to love her and feed her. But she has yet to understand that He sees much more in her, and she is going to have to stretch to grow into all He has for her as His queen.

Furthermore, she has yet to learn to say *yes* in her heart when it costs her something. He calls her out into a season of counting the cost of love. This is the season of laying it down to find Him above all things. John of the Cross described this as the journey of the "dark night of the soul" where love leads to the stripping away of all other attachments for the sake of being nearer to the lover.[1]

Jesus is calling the Bride to new heights of love, to leave the cozy place, and to come to the mountaintops. We read her words depicting this, "My beloved spoke, and said to me: 'Rise up, my love, my fair one, and come away'" (Song of Sol. 2:10). He wants to give her more of Himself, to show her life from a higher perspective. He wants to share His heart with her and enlarge her vision and capacity to receive His love. But she likes the place where she is. She tells Him to go, but she stays (see Song of Sol. 2:17). She says something like, "You go ahead, Jesus. I'll just stay here and wait for You. This is a nice comfortable place. I'm blessed and fulfilled. I'm happy here. But You go right on ahead if You want."

In this place, the Bride doesn't yet have a vision for the things that really burn on the Bridegroom's heart. Life is all about her, and she thinks it's good that way. The Bridegroom, on the other hand, is saying, "There is more, but you have to follow to get it."

Much of the Church lives where the Shulamite does. God's will is often interpreted as being the things which bless us the most and cost us the least. So many are willing to manipulate circumstances, spin the story line, and do the things that make them look good and attract people, but they aren't yet willing to die! Where are those who are asking, "What is it that You want?" or who are crying out like Jeremiah to hear the counsel of the Lord (see Jer. 23:18)?

In this stage of the story, the Bridegroom is calling the Bride out of the "it's all about me and what I want" perspective into the "it's all about the King and what He wants" perspective. He then leaves her to her own desires. He withdraws to the mountains. She can't feel His presence and longing begins to give birth to voluntary love on another level. She begins to feel the Psalm 63:1 craving in her soul, where she thirsts for Him "in a dry and thirsty land."

It's the presence of the Lord that makes our state of being come alive with value, life, joy, and contentment. Even the worst circumstances yield His life and comfort when His presence draws near and we know He is leading us. What seemed like an oasis when the King was near feels like a desert when He departs! So the cozy place the Bride had enjoyed, now void of His presence, becomes a dry and thirsty land. Her soul begins to ache for Him, and this longing gives way to pursuit as she says:

By night on my bed I sought the one I love; I sought him, but I did not find him. "I will rise now," I said, "and go about the city; in the streets and in the squares I will seek the one I love." I sought him, but I did not find him. The watchmen who go about the city found me; I said, "Have you seen the one I love?" Scarcely had I passed by them, when I found the one I love. I held him and would not let him go, until I had brought him to the house of my mother, and into the chamber of her who conceived me (Song of Solomon 3:1-4).

She fully abandons herself to love. She can't live in the status quo. She can't do the service without the substance of His presence in her life. Her comfort ceases to be her main concern. Instead, being with Him is now her main concern. This is all about going to the cross with her plans, goals, and life. And with that she declares, "Until the day breaks and the shadows flee away, I will go my way to the mountain of myrrh and to the hill of frankincense" (Song of Sol. 4:6).

Frankincense was offered in the temple with the meat sacrifice. It came to represent and be symbolic of prayer. Myrrh was one of the ingredients in the anointing oil for priests. It also was mingled with wine and offered to those who were condemned to be crucified. The mountain of myrrh and the hill of incense represent the cross. She is willing to give her life up as incense, to give herself to prayer, to be consumed by the fire of love. She is willing to take the partnership of suffering as well as the love that is better than wine. It's the laying down of her life, gladly, willingly, to enter into the fire of His heart. Now, she is willing to give it all.

This is the place He is calling a prophetic people to live. It's not about building a ministry or being seen by men, but rather it's the place of friendship; it's also the place of the cross. It's feeling His heart in its fullness. It's in getting His Word, feeling His burdens, and not loving our lives even unto death.

In this place of abandonment, our words won't be fashioned or determined by the fear or praise of men, but rather by His heart. It's a costly and difficult act, leaving the safe place, the status quo, the life where little is expected or risked. Yet it is in this place that the paradox of Christ's words, "whoever desires to save his life will lose it, but whoever loses his life for My sake will find it" (Matt. 16:25), actually make good sense. Our highest joy is found in His will. This is what love asks, and this is the choice the Bride makes.

And she is greatly rewarded for her choice. The Bridegroom comes to His Bride here and rewards her with a deeper fascination and knowledge of Him. He gives her a greater revelation of His power and glory, causing her to exclaim, "Who is this coming out of the wilderness like pillars of smoke, perfumed with myrrh and frankincense, with all the merchant's fragrant powders?" (Song of Sol. 3:6).

She had known Him in His love for her as a Bridegroom, but now she begins to understand another part of this Bridegroom. He is also a Mighty Warrior King who commands armies and rules with wisdom and glory. Her heart comes alive with the awesome revelation of what He is inviting her to be a part of. At this stage, where she has determined to give it all, even though her all feels small and inadequate, He again reaffirms His great love for her.

> *You are all fair, my love, and there is no spot in you.*
> *...You have ravished my heart, my sister, my spouse; you*
> *have ravished my heart with one look of your eyes, with*
> *one link of your necklace. How fair is your love, my sister,*
> *my spouse! How much better than wine is your love,*
> *and the scent of your perfumes than all spices!"* (Song of
> Solomon 4:7,9-10).

She is maturing in learning to see herself through His eyes, and her understanding of who He is opens her heart to long for more. Through the cross, the mountain of sacrifice, she is being healed as she is coming to know the depths of His love. She is amazed at His royalty and majesty, but is not quite to the place of seeing fully the destiny He has for her. She is an awestruck spectator as she watches Him come up from the wilderness. She is an abandoned lover at the edge of discovering her calling to rule and reign with Him. She doesn't yet understand it, but her weak adoration and prayers are paving heaven's interior with love and are filling the bowls with the fragrant incense of devotion.

> *He made its pillars of silver, its support of gold, its seat of purple, its interior paved with love by the daughters of Jerusalem* (Song of Solomon 3:10).

The Bride doesn't yet grasp the fullness of the effect of her petitions on the King, but He is so moved by her weak prayers. He will arise and answer.

STAGE THREE: MATURING IN BRIDAL PARTNERSHIP

In the third part of her journey, she begins to awaken to her partnership with the King in the release of His rule and reign in the earth. She is maturing in her position before Him and has consciously broken agreement with anything that hinders the flow of His love in her life. Out of mature love, she is learning to long for the things He longs for. When He calls, she eagerly answers. She won't go back to the old ways, because she knows there is nothing for her there. The best of her life is before her, not behind her. We find her saying:

> *I slept but my heart was awake. Listen! My beloved is knocking: "Open to me, my sister, my darling, my dove, my flawless one. My head is drenched with dew, my hair with the dampness of the night." I have taken off my robe—must I put it on again? I have washed my feet— must I soil them again? My beloved thrust his hand*

through the latch-opening; my heart began to pound for him. I arose to open for my beloved, and my hands dripped with myrrh, my fingers with flowing myrrh, on the handles of the bolt. I opened for my beloved, but my beloved had left; he was gone. My heart sank at his departure. I looked for him but did not find him. I called him but he did not answer. The watchmen found me as they made their rounds in the city. They beat me, they bruised me; they took away my cloak, those watchmen of the walls! (Song of Solomon 5:2-7 NIV)

She, now being fully devoted and confident in love, is even willing to endure persecution and ridicule for her Beloved. She won't look back to clothe herself with the garments stained by sin. She won't don the robes of the old ways anymore. She will no longer wear the sandals of the old paths. She is in love and ruined for sin. She only has eyes for Him. Though others may despise the fiery zeal of her love, she won't look back. Her heart is now beginning to be united with the things that burn on His heart. This is where the burden of the Lord begins to burn on our hearts as the Bride. Prophetic love arises, and we long to identify with what He sees and feels and speaks.

She goes down to the grove of trees to "look at the new growth in the valley, to see if the vines had budded or the pomegranates were in bloom. Before [she] realized it, [her] desire set [her] among the royal chariots of [her] people" (Song of Sol. 6:11-12 NIV). We see her heart is becoming fully immersed in her place as His queen. Love has made the things that burn in Him her main priorities. She has come a long way from those early days when all she wanted was to be pampered at the warmth of His fire. She is becoming a warrior queen, desiring to partner with Him in building and releasing His Kingdom and rule. She is looking for the harvest and wants to labor with Him in bringing it in. Thus, she says:

Come, my beloved, let us go forth to the field; let us lodge in the villages. Let us get up early to the vineyards; let us see if the vine has budded, whether the grape blossoms are open, and the pomegranates are in bloom. There I will give you my love. The mandrakes give off a fragrance, and at our gates are pleasant fruits, all manner, new and old, which I have laid up for you, my beloved (Song of Solomon 7:11-13).

She is now longing to be engaged with Him in His heart and His purpose. She is partnering with Him in the vineyards, feeling His heart. The full expression of passion and purpose has rightly met in her heart. His passionate, unchanging, and powerful love has given her confidence to walk out her purposes in and with Him. She has laid hold of her part in the testimony of Jesus. She has become a Psalm 84 pilgrim, releasing the life of the Spirit into the dry and hopeless places.

Blessed is the man whose strength is in You, whose heart is set on pilgrimage. As they pass through the Valley of Baca, they make it a spring; the rain also covers it with pools. They go from strength to strength; each one appears before God in Zion (Psalm 84:5-7).

So it is with a prophetic people. They are not ministry driven; they are love driven. Intimate love prevents burnout. Ministry calling cannot sustain our hearts. The needs that cry out to be met cannot sustain our hearts in labor. Only intimate love with the One who called us can also sustain us in that calling over the course of the journey. This is true for the Bride, and part of our prophetic call as friends of the Bridegroom is to encourage and release the Bride into this truth.

STAGE FOUR: STANDING IN FULLNESS

In the last stage of the story, the Bride has come into full maturity. Her life is given in love, and her Beloved gives the increase of anointing on her heart for love and on her hands for works. She is now pictured as one "leaning upon her beloved" (Song of Sol. 8:5). She is no longer a spectator watching Him come up. She now is willing to journey to the wilderness with Him. She is leaning on Him in love, confident that even in weakness, as she fully pursues Him, His love will grow and increase. She comes up with Him, ready to stand and be identified as being wholly His without shame. Her intercession comes from deeper intimacy, friendship, and commitment. Her outward cry is for the release of power to accomplish His purposes.

> *Place me like a seal over your heart, like a seal on your arm; for love is as strong as death, its jealousy unyielding as the grave. It burns like blazing fire, like a mighty flame* (Song of Solomon 8:6 NIV).

The seal on the heart is the sign of intimacy. In ancient times, some kings placed their signet ring on a chain and hung it around the neck of their bride, where it would rest over their heart. This signified that the king trusted his bride's heart and was willing to also trust her with his authority. We see here in Song of Solomon that the Bridegroom draws her into His heart with great love and affection, and then releases His power to release the Kingdom through her. Her cry in response is to live close to His heart and to be a channel of His blessing in the earth. The seal on her heart is the branding of His love. The seal on her arm is the exercise of His right arm of power. The more she humbly and gratefully lives in love, the greater the release of His power.

Additionally, there is a mutual jealousy. He is jealous over her destiny, and she is jealous for His name in the earth and longs to represent Him rightly in holiness, love, and power. This is the picture of the mature Bride, standing in prophetic power and authority at the end of the age. This is where we are going. This is the mandate of prophetic messengers. We are to be marked with intimacy and authority to prepare the Bride to be her greatest in that day. Neither fiery trials nor floodwaters of attacks can extinguish the flame of love in the heart that burns for Him.

> *Many waters cannot quench love; rivers cannot sweep it away. If one were to give all the wealth of one's house for love, it would be utterly scorned* (Song of Solomon 8:7 NIV).

IN SUMMARY

The main reason a healthy knowledge of the Father's heart and the Bridal Paradigm are important in the prophetic is that they lay a right foundation for confidence in ministry. The knowledge that the Father wants to lavish His affections on me, that He is completely on my side and has a good purpose for my life, enables and encourages me to step out in faith in the exercise of my gifts and my call. I don't have to walk in the fear that, if I miss it or make a mistake, He is going to take me out of the game. He may discipline me in love, but He won't kick me off the team.

Likewise, knowing that Jesus is a passionate Bridegroom who is dedicated to my success and longs for me with a deep, fiery love strengthens and equips me to stay faithful in the mundane and the difficulties of daily life. I am not a success because I am good at ministry. I am successful because I am His friend and my Father's child. If I don't give up, I win.

Finally, as I surrender my life to His desires and purposes in the earth, I lay a right foundation that will help me prophesy from right motives and with the right perspective of how God sees people.

Having laid a foundation, let's look at a few things we can do to cultivate a prophetic spirit in us. By *prophetic spirit*, I mean an ear to hear His voice, an eye to see His hand, and a heart/mouth connection to speak His words. It's about learning to encounter God and go deep in His heart.

GETTING PLUGGED IN

1. Spend the next week praying through Song of Solomon 2:14. Sing it over yourself. Speak it over yourself. Ask Jesus as your Bridegroom King to talk to you about what it means to be hidden in the cleft of the rock. What is He thinking when He calls you His dove? Let your heart be moved by the phrase, "Your face is beautiful and your voice is sweet."

2. Consider the four stages of the maturity of the Bride. What stage do you think you are in, and how can you mature more deeply in that level or move to the next?

3. Ask the Lord to show you someone who needs to hear this verse. Ask for a word to give them along with this Scripture to encourage them.

NOTE

1. John of the Cross, *The Essential Writings* (New York: Harper One, 2004) 4.

Chapter Six

CULTIVATING A PROPHETIC SPIRIT

WE MAY UNDERSTAND THE CONCEPTS OF INTIMACY IN OUR HEADS, but we need to appropriate them into our hearts. In Western culture, we are not accustomed to viewing life as a journey in God, where it takes time and longing and energy to dig out the beauty and wisdom of His nature, His love, and His very Being on a day-to-day basis. We like the most complicated concepts to be boiled down into something we can understand in ten minutes or less, and we want spiritual gifts and maturity to flow through us mightily starting yesterday. The last time I checked I didn't see a *spiritual maturity* button on my microwave oven menu. Life is a journey, and intimacy with God is developed on the journey as we make Him our journey's goal.

A LIFE OF PRAYER

Of the many things I have found to be most helpful on the journey, building intimacy through a life of prayer is at the top of the list. I like to use the phrase *life of prayer* for two reasons. First, it is not a *prayer life*, but a whole, entire life of prayer. A *prayer life* sometimes carries the connotation of a starting and stopping time. Maybe ten minutes here, an hour there. I completely subscribe to having a daily time set apart with God in the secret place. Many of the keys I will be discussing will take place in the context of a set apart time. But I want to do away with the idea of *our time* and *His time*, and the idea that it all takes place in a time marked *start* and *finish*. God is always near us, wanting to share His secrets, taking us into His confidence, and sharing His affections with us. Our little thirty-second prayers or songs or offerings of praise throughout the day are real to God, and they move His heart. They also keep us aware of His presence throughout our days.

Second, I like to start with the word *life*, because it is in this fellowship that the foundations of our lives are built and established. The word *prayer*, when disconnected from *life*, carries a lot of baggage with it. People have many negative associations with the word *prayer*. Words like *dry, boring, hard,* and *dull* are often used to describe prayer. Prayer is one of those things we are told we have to do, and it's part of the Christian life. We have been told and retold by our pastors and spiritual mentors that it's necessary. So we grit our teeth and force ourselves to endure it. Yet God said that He wanted to give us joy in His house of prayer. His intent is for us to find strength and joy and life in the place of prayer, as we read in Isaiah 56:7.

> *These I will bring to my holy mountain and give them joy in my house of prayer. Their burnt offerings and sacrifices will be accepted on my altar; for my house will be called a house of prayer for all nations* (NIV).

In the journey of building the life of prayer, our identity in God is established. In fact, the primary identity and calling of every believer is to first be with God and then, out of that relationship, exercise authority in ruling with Him.

When Jesus came in the flesh, Mark tells us that He called disciples who would be with Him and whom He would send out: "He appointed twelve that they might be with him and that he might send them out to preach and to have authority to drive out demons" (Mark 3:14-15 NIV).

They had to be with Him, to know Him, before He sent them out to bring and release Kingdom authority and power. The apostle John understood this even in connection with the purpose of our redemption. He was caught up into heaven where he heard the angels, creatures, and elders all sing of the worthiness of the Lamb to receive praise because He purchased people from every nation to be kings and priests unto God. He was so taken by this revelation that he wove it into his introduction to his book, repeating again in it that we were purchased by the blood of Christ to be a kingdom of priests before God. He says:

> *And from Jesus Christ, who is the faithful witness, the firstborn from the dead, and the ruler of the kings of the earth. To him who loves us and has freed us from our sins by his blood, and has made us to be a kingdom and priests to serve his God and Father—to him be glory and power for ever and ever! Amen* (Revelation 1:5-6 NIV).

We are called to stand before Him as priests in governmental authority. This role is to be exercised by every believer in the place of prayer where, as worshipers and intercessors, we are filling heaven with our love, adoration, and worship. Here we exercise authority and release God's power and will from the greatest governmental center in the universe, His throne room, where we are seated in Christ. The emphasis here is not on the calling *to do*, but the calling *to be*. John didn't hear heaven say that we were purchased *to be* teachers and prophets and apostles. He didn't say we were purchased *to be* musicians or ushers or deacons. All these are callings or ministry expressions that are released first out of the context of relationship. It's the reflection of the First and Second Commandments, our role as priest falling under the first command to love God with everything in us, and our ministry assignments falling into the second command where we release our authority, calling, and gifting in the context of loving our neighbor and spreading the gospel.

In the wisdom of God, He has given a pattern that everyone can embrace—young and old, male and female, highly gifted or slightly gifted. We can see it in Ephesians 1:17, where Paul prays for the Church to have the Spirit of wisdom and revelation so she might know Him, Jesus, on an intimate level. Out of this relationship comes the rest of his prayer:

> *The eyes of your understanding being enlightened; that you may know what is the hope of His calling, what are the riches of the glory of His inheritance in the saints, and what is the exceeding greatness of His power toward us who believe* (Ephesians 1:18-19).

Out of our growing intimacy with Christ, we find that the eyes of our hearts become increasingly enlightened to know the hope of our calling (eternal and temporal), the inheritance in Him that we are to possess, and the experience of the greater power leading to the greater works and the ability to fulfill our calling and possess the land He has called us to take.

God wants our identities to be established in and through our relationship with Him, not our works for Him. Yes, we were created before the foundations of the earth to do good works in the Kingdom of God, but the works are designed to come as the overflow and outgrowth of our inward fellowship with Him. Works and gifts are only "icing on the cake" of the fact that we love Him and are loved by Him. Spiritual gifts that are emphasized in the vacuum of an ongoing, growing spiritual relationship with Christ will often lead people astray. This is why Jesus will say to some on that day, *"I never knew you. Away from me, you evildoers"* (Matt. 7:23 NIV).

When our identity gets wrapped up in our prophetic gifting, things will begin to unravel. We will find ourselves jealous of those more highly gifted, or offended because we aren't being recognized, or confused when God calls us into seasons of hiddenness. He is so jealous for us and has designed us to find our identities in His presence and love, not in our own callings and abilities. This is why the development of a life of prayer is so key to a solid prophetic lifestyle. It is in being before His face that we come to know His affections over us and His desire for us. Here, we receive the grace and confidence that, even when we are weak and broken, He still loves and enjoys us. Understanding these truths in relationship with Him makes us unshakeable when our outer circumstances shift and change in different seasons of life.

CHANGING OUR PERSPECTIVE ON PRAYER

So how does prayer become enjoyable? First, we must understand that God wants us to be before Him, not because it's our duty but because He enjoys us. When you pray, He answers. He wants to give you wisdom and revelation. He wants to open up the Scriptures to you. He desires to fan the flame of love in your heart with the fire that He is. He is not distant, and He is not grading you on the time, eloquence, or content of your prayers.

I have had people say to me, "Oh, our little house of prayer is only doing eighteen hours a week," as if it weren't important because they aren't 24/7 like IHOP-KC. Abba is so excited about that "little 18 hours." He is not saying, "Do more, and you will be better." He is smiling and saying, "You are doing eighteen hours a week! That's awesome!" So, individually, He is not setting a time when you start and judging how good your fellowship with Him was by how long you talked! He loves spending time with you.

Can you imagine a husband setting a kitchen timer on the table and hitting *start* to begin a conversation with his wife? "Okay, honey. We have been talking ten minutes now; only five more to go, and our conversation will be done!" For two people in love, the quality isn't weighed in time, but rather communion. Now granted, it takes time for people to connect, and we aren't going to develop intimacy with God on the run, rarely spending time in the Word or in focused interchange. But we aren't to approach the time investment from the perspective of duty, but rather from that of love and the expectation of communion.

We aren't to simply see our prayer investment as satisfying today's requirement, but rather the building of an equity of love and fellowship over a lifetime. If I came home and said to my wife, "Okay, honey. I am ready to perform my communication duty with you, so sit down at the table and we can start talking, but let's get this done because I have other things to do," I would find myself in a one-sided conversation, because I would be the only one left at the table! I fall more in love with Jesus when we converse together. How do we do that?

The foundation of intimacy is built on the confidence that He desires us. This is the essence of the Father's heart and Bridal Paradigm. When I know He loves me all the time, I don't waste time at the front end of communion trying to climb out of guilt, condemnation, or shame in order to be clean and prepared to fellowship with God. Many Christians are always trying to climb out of darkness, hoping to live in the light, when they are already, by virtue of the cross, in the light.

We aren't earning our way into the light by our good behavior. We are in the light because, through the blood of Jesus, light is our abode. When we get out of the light, we need to repent, press delete on darkness, and get back in the light. The knowledge that He takes pleasure in me releases the confidence and joy in the place of prayer, as we learned in our discussion of the Bridal Paradigm.

Without a doubt, the one thing over the years that has set me with confidence in Abba's love is the practice of praying Scripture. I have prayed through Psalms, Proverbs, some of the prophets, some of the Gospels, and many of the NT letters. I do this with one goal—that I might know Him both in the Word and the Spirit. Granted, not every biblical book completely lends itself to this purpose, but you would be surprised how much there is to pray. Even if the whole book isn't conducive to be prayed, many portions are. How many times have you read a passage of Scripture and said to yourself, "Oh, this is so good"? Maybe you even asked the Lord to work into your heart the very thing you loved about it. Take it a step further and pray it.

Praying the Word has so many advantages. First, you always have something in front of you to pray. You don't have to sit and wonder how to talk to God; it's already right there in front of your eyes. You can finish your conversation with God in one place, and the next day come right back to the next passage and start your conversation right where you left off.

A second thing about praying Scripture is that, when your mind begins to wander, you have a place to come back to. When you begin to wander into your to-do list for the day and realize your concentration is slipping, you can come back to the passage before you and start again. Some days I have to do this several times before I actually really begin to connect, but it is so worth it. There are times that, if I didn't have the Word to come back to, I would spend all my prayer time fixing things around the house and solving all the world's problems in my mind!

Growing in sanctification is a third reason to pray the word. Paul said in Romans 12 that we are not to be conformed to the world's pattern, but rather we are to be transformed by the renewing of our minds. When we pray Scripture we are eating from the table of God's thoughts, desires, and will. The Holy Spirit takes these times to transform our minds and increase our revelation of who He is and how He sees us. In partnership with our wills and the *yes*es in our hearts, He powerfully transforms us to be more like Him in our emotions, wills, and affections. I have found at times as I prayed through particular passages that I carried wrong views about myself that separated me from Him. Praying the truths of His Word over my mind and heart brought healing, transformation, and a greater measure of sanctification. I believe this is connected to that process of growing from glory to glory that Paul speaks of in Second Corinthians 3:18. Also, in this communion with God in the Word, our hearts become softer and more pliable. When a passage we are praying through convicts us of sin, we are quicker to confess and repent because we want to live life in a way that is more pleasing to Him. Over time, we can't help but become more conformed to His image in the sanctification process.

A fourth reason to pray Scripture is that it's key to developing your prophetic gifting. When you pray the Word, you are storing up prophetic oil that will come out of you when you prophesy. Even if it isn't Scripture verbatim, the foundation of the Word will be interwoven with the words you give to others. I have, and I'm sure you have as well, heard and even received so many prophetic words that are hollow, fluffy, flattering, or completely disconnected from the heart of God's Word. Praying Scripture builds integrity into your life that can't help but come through in the prophetic words that you give to others. I tell all those in the classes I teach that, if they will go deep in praying the Word, they will never lack for something to prophesy!

The last reason, and my absolute favorite, is that praying Scripture teaches me to fellowship with the Holy Spirit and encounter Abba's heart and mind through the very means that He has divinely chosen to communicate with me. There is nothing like having the One who wrote the Word come and explain it to you. There is nothing like drinking at the fountain of the Spirit by means of His explaining to you exactly what Jesus means when He looks at you and says, "Let me see your face and let me hear your voice. Your face is beautiful to Me, and your voice is sweet to Me." It doesn't get any better than that! For me, these places of communion have been the foundation of the deepest encounters I have had with God.

When the Holy Spirit invites us to go deep into the heart of the Father through the path of the Word, He is laying the foundation for the joy of encounter. And this should change our perspective on prayer being dull, boring, dry, or anything other than enjoyable!

PRAYING SCRIPTURE

There have been several formulas for praying or meditating on Scripture over the years, going back, of course, to the OT saints. Isaac spent time meditating on God. We read in Genesis 24:63, "And Isaac went out to meditate in the field in the evening."

Moses told the Israelites to keep the Word in front of them all the time, in whatever they were doing or wherever they were going. Furthermore, he commanded the people to meditate on the words and commands of God.

> *Hear, O Israel: The Lord our God, the Lord is one. Love the Lord your God with all your heart and with all your soul and with all your strength. These commandments that I give you today are to be on your hearts. Impress them on your children. Talk about them when you sit at home and when you walk along the road, when you lie down and when you get up. Tie them as symbols on your hands, and bind them on your foreheads. Write them on the doorframes of your houses and on your gates* (Deuteronomy 6:4-9 NIV).

The singers of Psalm 119 all cried out with desire for God's Word to be written in their hearts and thoughts. They proclaimed:

I meditate on your precepts and consider your ways. I delight in your decrees; I will not neglect your word (Psalm 119:15-16 NIV).

For I delight in your commands because I love them. I reach out for your commands, which I love, that I may meditate on your decrees (Psalm 119:47-48 NIV).

How sweet are your words to my taste, sweeter than honey to my mouth! I gain understanding from your precepts; therefore I hate every wrong path (Psalm 119:103-104 NIV).

The prophet Jeremiah exclaimed, "Your words were found, and I ate them, and Your word was to me the joy and rejoicing of my heart" (Jer. 15:16). The apostle Paul echoed these same thoughts when he said:

Let the message of Christ dwell among you richly as you teach and admonish one another with all wisdom through psalms, hymns, and songs from the Spirit, singing to God with gratitude in your hearts (Colossians 3:16 NIV).

Whether we acknowledge it or not, we all have a *heavenly GPS* in our spirit, and it's always calling us upward. Throughout the history of the Church, there have been men and women who have sought the deepest communion possible with God on this side of heaven. The study of the mystics continually inspires me in my pursuit of deeper communion. Their hunger and ways of pursuing that goal have aided me in developing my own style of praying Scripture. Much of my methodology is a composite of my own trial and error, as well as an adaptation of some of the ways of the ancients. I am sharing my method here, but I encourage you to experiment and find out what works for you. If it seems awkward at first, just stay with it. As you become more comfortable and you begin to encounter Him more regularly in praying the Word, you will wonder why you never tried it before.

PREPARING OUR HEARTS TO SEEK HIM: PRACTICING HIS PRESENCE

In an earlier chapter, I mentioned the three tenets of mystical theology, which simply state that 1) God exists, 2) God is personal, and 3) God desires personal communion with every human being. I would describe my own version of this as what I call *a theology of His presence*. By that, I simply mean that I want to continually grow in the knowledge and sensitivity to the constant presence of God around me.

When I am growing in this understanding, a life of prayer becomes a more realistic and reachable concept. He is always present. Waking, sleeping, driving, working, at the soccer field or basketball court, in my conversations with others or when I am alone, His presence never leaves. The Holy Spirit lives inside of us. He doesn't leave when we engage in activities that are secular. Realizing that He is a breath away encourages our hearts to learn to live in a posture of presence.

Another thought that captures me in connection with learning to live in His presence is the connection of prayer with eternity. God is the substance of eternity. Eternity is filled with the fullness of the Being and attributes of God. Prayer, even in a thirty-second format, is a foray into eternity because there is no time with God. A simple, "I love You, Jesus," is a short step into His timeless presence. Though we are often aware of the clock, God is not. He is always "I Am."

Jesus said that they who believe have eternal life (see John 5:24; 6:47). That life is real, now, and we can step into a piece of that life every time we stop to meditate, pause, and think about Him. Prayer is like breathing in eternity. It's like stepping into the fullness of God's Being for however long we engage. This is where we taste of heavenly things. This is where we go to that place that Paul spoke of when he said to think on the things above (see Col. 3:1-2).

When we pray, we are stepping into eternity to affect eternity in the *now* and to affect the *now* for eternity. It is real, and it makes a difference. Our weak prayers in His presence move the God of eternity and, therefore, affect eternity. Oh, the wisdom of God and the simplicity and wonder of prayer. Understanding that He is near, actually waiting and inviting me to talk to Him and with Him, prepares my heart for conversation around His Word.

PREPARING OUR HEARTS TO SEEK HIM: PRAYING IN THE HOLY SPIRIT

Two scriptures that I briefly want to touch on are:

> *For anyone who speaks in a tongue does not speak to people but to God. Indeed, no one understands them; they utter mysteries by the Spirit. But the one who prophesies speaks to people for their strengthening, encouraging and comfort* (1 Corinthians 14:2-3 NIV).

> *In the same way, the Spirit helps us in our weakness. We do not know what we ought to pray for, but the Spirit himself intercedes for us through wordless groans* (Romans 8:26 NIV).

Paul spoke in tongues. Peter spoke in tongues. The disciples spoke in tongues. Speaking in tongues, according to Paul, allows our spirits to commune deeply with the Holy Spirit. There is a mysterious divine exchange that happens when we pray in the Spirit. Though we don't understand it, there is an edifying factor that praying in the Spirit produces on the inside.

When I pray in the Spirit, my heart is being tenderized and my spirit is aligning with God's Spirit. Paul expresses this in the Romans passage, though he takes it deeper to include groanings, which again are a spiritual exchange between our spirits and the

Spirit of God. Paul makes it plain. Sometimes, we just don't know how to pray, but the Holy Spirit always knows how to pray through us, so He groans through us and those groans connect us to and release us in the will of God. Paul groaned in the Spirit and spoke in tongues to the extent that he told the Corinthians he prayed in tongues more than all of them did (see 1 Cor. 14:18). There was a reason he did so—it connected his spirit deeply to God. Praying in the Spirit connects our spirits to the Spirit of God. Praying in the Spirit for a while is good preparation for taking the next step to pray Scripture.

PRAYING THE WORD: WHERE TO BEGIN

Begin by choosing a book of the Bible to start with. If this is new to you, Psalms is a good place to begin because they are already written prayers and songs.

I like to stay with a book until I finish praying all the way through it. The benefit of staying with a book is the continuity you develop by praying through it. You not only gain insight into the Word, but you also gain insight into the author's relationship with God. I have come to regard David, Jeremiah, and John as good friends. I gained insight into God's heart through their experiences with Him.

Write the passage out (or type it). Say it out loud to God. Sing it, if it helps you receive it more. Remember, the goal of this practice is to know Jesus more, so don't aim at quantity. If you start praying and get so locked into one verse that you spend all your time there, so be it. I love it when that happens. Just pick up the next day where you left off.

Remember that the goal is the heart connect between you, the Word, and the Spirit. We don't want information; we want communion, so ask Abba lots of questions. He loves it!

Some of the deepest, most personal times of revelation and encounter have come when I have entered into conversations with

Him that started with a question. A few years back I was praying through Revelation 4. Verse three describes God as one sitting on the throne whose appearance was like sardius and jasper. I asked the Lord, "What does this look like?" I paused to look up *sardius* and *jasper* so I could try to piece it together. Sardius is a red stone, kind of like a ruby, and jasper is a translucent stone, similar to a diamond. I imagined this fiery God on a throne with a ruby in front of Him and a diamond in front of the ruby. Then I imagined a billion-watt light bulb shining through them from the throne. What I saw was a dancing, undefinable, uncontainable fire. It was so real to me that I was immediately caught up in the fear of the Lord. Passages from Isaiah 33 and 57 flooded my mind.

> *Who of us can dwell with the consuming fire? Who of us can dwell with everlasting burning?* (Isaiah 33:14 NIV)

> *For this is what the high and exalted One says—he who lives forever, whose name is holy: "I live in a high and holy place, but also with the one who is contrite and lowly in spirit, to revive the spirit of the lowly and to revive the heart of the contrite"* (Isaiah 57:15 NIV).

My sense, in the fear of the Lord, was, "How do I rightly approach You?" Believe me, it wasn't a theological question. He is so beautiful and holy and majestic and awesome. As I sat in the presence of the Lord, the Holy Spirit spoke to me through Ephesians 1:

> *Blessed be the God and Father of our Lord Jesus Christ, who has blessed us with every spiritual blessing in the heavenly places in Christ, just as He chose us in Him before the foundation of the world, that we should be holy and without blame before Him in love, having predestined us to adoption as sons by Jesus Christ to Himself* (Ephesians 1:3-5).

He said, "In the heart of this fiery, all-consuming, all-powerful God dwells the heart of a Father who has longed to fellowship with you since before the foundations of the earth." I wept at such a revelation of love. My heart was undone that He wanted me! From all eternity, I have been in His Father-heart and He delightfully chose me as a son. This sweet revelation came to me just because I asked God a question about what He looked like in Revelation 4. So, now, I always ask questions about Scripture when I am not getting its meaning. I'll say things like, "Holy Spirit, come and teach me," or "Abba, what was David thinking when he wrote this?" I am amazed at how the Teacher wants to reveal Himself to me.

The following is a simple example of how to meditate through a passage, using Psalm 139:13-18 as an exercise in praying the word. As I previously said, I would first write it out.

> For you created my inmost being; you knit me together in my mother's womb. I praise you because I am fearfully and wonderfully made; your works are wonderful, I know that full well. My frame was not hidden from you when I was made in the secret place, when I was woven together in the depths of the earth. Your eyes saw my unformed body; all the days ordained for me were written in your book before one of them came to be. How precious to me are your thoughts, God! How vast is the sum of them! Were I to count them, they would outnumber the grains of sand—when I awake, I am still with you (NIV).

Begin by thanking Him for speaking to you. Pray in the Spirit, asking Him to open God's Word to you. Jesus promised that the Holy Spirit would do this for us. He said:

> I still have many things to say to you, but you cannot bear them now. However, when He, the Spirit of truth, has come, He will guide you into all truth; for He will

not speak on His own authority, but whatever He hears He will speak; and He will tell you things to come. He will glorify Me, for He will take of what is Mine and declare it to you. All things that the Father has are Mine. Therefore I said that He will take of Mine and declare it to you (John 16:12-15).

After reading the passage, what concepts, words or phrases of the psalm passage speak or stand out to you? Ask Him questions about these areas. Put yourself in the story line. Place your imagination at the service of prayer, picturing the scene or characters, putting yourself in their places, conversing with God in the process. For example:

For you created my inmost being; you knit me together in my mother's womb. I praise you because I am fearfully and wonderfully made; your works are wonderful, I know that full well. My frame was not hidden from you when I was made in the secret place, when I was woven together in the depths of the earth. Your eyes saw my unformed body.

Here are a few questions and thoughts that come to mind regarding this passage. "Abba, You were there when I was created. What did You think about me? What was in Your heart when You saw me come into being? What did You feel? What songs were You singing over me? You say I am fearfully and wonderfully made. You liked me in my mother's womb! You planned every detail about my physical being. Thank You for how You made me. I come out of agreement with any lie of the enemy regarding my beauty or value. You love me as I am!"

And when praying the following line, "And in Your book they all were written, the days fashioned for me, when as yet there were none of them," I can begin to declare, "Thank You for writing me into Your story line. You gave me a testimony and destined me for impact. You made me to be great for You and to make a difference. You have a good plan, and You are a good leader over my life."

The next lines of the psalm say, "How precious also are Your thoughts to me, O God! How great is the sum of them! If I should count them, they would be more in number than the sand." To this, I could respond, "Oh, how You love me! You think about me all the time, good things. And Your thoughts toward me are greater than the sands of the sea. You desire to bless and enjoy me. You love the sound of my voice. What are some of those thoughts You think about me right now?"

And what a comfort to know that "when I awake, I am still with You." But before I sleep, I can ask, "Abba, would You speak to me in my dreams? Come to me in my sleep and fellowship with me. Thank You that You are always with me, awake or asleep, that You are there watching over me."

Converse with Him from your heart and mind. Stop often and pause. Listen for Him to speak to you through impressions, words, pictures, or other related scriptures. When you get something, great or small, respond with thanksgiving and ask for more. Wait and respond. Praise and worship Him for the revelation of who He is and what He is showing you.

What are the things that you don't understand about this passage? Ask Him to explain those things, too, and give you a spirit of revelation on them.

You also want to think about how to apply what He is speaking to you into your daily life. What does this look like practically? (For example, "Lord, help me to see myself the way You see me. Touch my eyes. Touch my heart.") Prophesy over yourself by declaring the truths you are meditating on over your own heart.

As you wind down this time with Him around the Word, resolve to submit anything to Him that He requires from you, and ask for grace for deeper obedience.

Conclude your time by journaling your dialogue as a continuation of prayer. Write your thoughts and revelation in a continuation of conversational prayer—directly talking to God and making declarations, resolutions, and requests (For example, "Thank You, Jesus, for showing me the depth of Your love for me. Help me give my heart to You and to be aware of Your presence more fully.") As you journal, you will often receive more while you write.

There are a few things that are helpful to keep in mind. Keep a Bible dictionary and a regular dictionary nearby. When you come across a word that is unclear to you or a biblical name or place you don't recognize, look it up. The Holy Spirit isn't going to go away while you pause to gain deeper understanding. Once you have the definition, enter back into conversation with Abba.

Abba is a real Father. Jesus is at the right hand of the Father. The Holy Spirit is an indwelling presence and teacher. The Trinity loves to engage us in conversation about what He has written to us. He won't go away while we look up a word.

Some days will seem to be full of revelation, while other days will seem harder to engage. That's part of the journey. Always take time to journal what you get, even if it is only a thought or two. It's all spiritual food, and even if you don't feel like you got anything on that day, it all adds up. Days turn to weeks, weeks turn to months, and months turn to years. I guarantee, if you stay with this, you will grow deep in the intimate knowledge of God. Your life and gifts and ministry will overflow with His blessing.

GETTING PLUGGED IN

1. Ask the Holy Spirit to encourage you and remind you of the presence of Abba around you throughout your day. At the end of the day, reflect on the difference it made over your day. Ask the Lord to increase your sense of His presence throughout your week.

2. Choose a book of the Bible to begin praying this week. Commit to praying Scripture at least fifteen minutes a day. Don't forget to journal. At the end of the week, reflect upon any changes in your ability to hear God's voice.

3. Take the passage or word that you were most impressed with and ask the Lord to give you a prophetic word for someone built around that passage.

Chapter Seven

KEYS TO CULTIVATING A PROPHETIC SPIRIT

ONE OF THE THINGS I SEE INCREASINGLY ABSENT IN THE LIVES OF believers is the sheer fascination with the Person of God. Learning to live *fascinated with God* will maintain our hearts in a place of revelation and wonder. Jesus was always blowing the disciples' minds. When they thought they had Him figured out, He would do something that would completely confound them. Take, for example, when a storm arose on the lake and waves began to enter the boat. The disciples began to fear for their lives, so they woke up Jesus. After He spoke to the sea and the wind, everything was immediately calm. The disciples looked at each other in utter amazement. Mark 4:41 says, "And they feared exceedingly, and said to one another, 'Who can this be, that even the wind and the sea obey Him!'"

I wonder how many times, in the three years they were with Him, they asked each other that question, "Who is this guy?" That's fascination! That's wonder! The Western church has done a great job of perfecting doctrine and practice. We have the Sunday morning service down to a science. We know how to get the most out of our time, have the best music, and share the most palatable messages. I fear that, in our attempts to define and explain God, we have removed the *fascination factor*. In our need for mental explanation and understanding, have we created a God we can control and explain?

There is a deeper hunger within us, but we aren't sure how to satisfy it, so we end up filling it with other things, yet there is a thirst that still remains unquenched. Gazing on the beauty of God in praying the Word can open up the wonder and mystery to us on a regular basis. This leads us to deeper fascination, which regularly renews first love and reminds us why we fell in love with Him in the first place.

FASCINATED BY THE MYSTERY OF GOD

Recently, I was praying through Mark, and I came to the passage on the Great Commandment. When I asked the Lord how I could love Him with all my mind, He impressed on me to do this by looking at His intelligence expressed in creation. The first thing I thought of was the fact that all of creation is sustained by His voice. There is creative power in His voice. Then, I thought of how He created me with a voice and that I have a unique set of sound waves comprising my voice—that there is no other voice in the universe with the same voiceprint as mine. I thought of Song of Solomon 2:14, how to Him my voice is sweet. I realized that when I speak to Him, out of all the millions of voices in the earth, He recognizes my voiceprint and, when I pray, He responds to it.

This reveals the power of the prophetic word in a different light. When I hear His voice and speak on His behalf, there is an anointing and authority on my voice. He designed it this way, where there is a literal power on an authentic word of God that is carried through our voices. This revelation fascinated my spirit but also made me love Him with my mind. Divine intelligence drew this response from me.

This rich feast came by my simply asking God a question about something He commanded me to do! Staying tuned in to the wonder and mystery of God cultivates within me a prophetic spirit because it keeps me close to the heart of God as opposed to allowing me to just be preoccupied with the gift. It keeps the element of the mystery of God connected to the mystery of the prophetic.

Jeremiah told the Israelites to choose the ancient paths. He declared the word of the Lord which was, "Stand in the ways and see; and ask for the old paths, where the good way is, and walk in it; then you will find rest for your souls" (Jer. 6:16).

The ancients understood that the depths and the richness of God are way beyond a momentary pursuit. They are an eternal pursuit. There is always more of God, and the more we lean into Him, the more we cultivate a tender spirit with which to hear His amazing voice! I like the way St. Francis de Sales puts it.

> There is more in God's infinity than we will ever observe or experience. Fish can enjoy the astonishing immensity of an ocean. But no fish has ever seen it all. Birds fly through the air, but no bird has flown everywhere...our souls will swim in the ocean and fly in the atmosphere of Divinity, but there will always remain infinitely more of God. The blessed spirits will be thrilled by two observations: the infinite beauty they contemplate and the chasm of infinity that remains to be seen.[1]

As our hearts are awakened to the beauty, wonder, and mystery of this God who so loves us, our spirits are more open to the revelation of His mysteries as we grow in the gift of prophecy. Paul makes a connection between prophecy and receiving revelation of divine mysteries. He says, "And though I have the gift of prophecy, and understand all mysteries and all knowledge…but have not love, I am nothing" (1 Cor. 13:2).

Paul's point in the passage is the supremacy of love in operating in gifts of the spirit; however, as we grow in love and the prophetic, we will prophecy the mysteries and knowledge of God. As Wayne Grudem states:

> Nevertheless, this passage does make clear by implication that knowing "mysteries" and "knowledge," even if only in part, is a normal component of the gift of prophecy…."Mysteries" here are "the secret thoughts, plans, and dispensations of God which are hidden from the human reason…and hence must be revealed to those for whom they are intended."[2]

A LIFESTYLE OF WORSHIP

Another by-product of fellowshipping with the Holy Spirit through praying Scripture is we grow in a lifestyle of worship. This is more than attending a church service or singing some devotional songs in a home Bible study. This is part of learning to pray without ceasing and is expressed through intentionally abiding in Christ and fellowshipping with the Holy Spirit.

Jude commanded the saints, "Keep yourselves in the love of God, looking for the mercy of our Lord Jesus Christ unto eternal life" (Jude 21). This is a way to learn to keep our sails up by keeping our hearts and spirits in tune with Jesus. Jesus said, "God is Spirit, and those who worship Him must worship in spirit and truth" (John 4:24).

God is inviting us to walk in a lifestyle of adoration and thanksgiving throughout the day. Many think that, if they aren't engaged in intense intercession or worship, their prayers aren't powerful. The truth is, it all counts before the Lord, whether we are in the prayer meeting for an hour or whether we are driving our cars and whispering a simple "I love You, Jesus" every time we think of Him.

I had a dream where I was able to see beyond the veil where people were praying and speaking in tongues. On earth's side, people were feeling weak and like their prayers weren't very anointed. As their prayers went heavenward and they passed through the veil, they went off like fireworks. The angels rejoiced and were empowered. In my dream, it was as if their prayers released divine assignments as Abba sent this one here and that one there. He breathed in their prayers like sweet-smelling incense and appeared to exude a sense of pleasure and thankfulness to the Bride for carrying His burden of prayer in the earth.

The times we learn to pause to love Jesus, and through the Holy Spirit drink in and receive the affections of Abba, will cause us to regularly connect with the heart of God in a worshipful way.

As His friends who learn to walk in adoration and thanksgiving, we are the ones who will hear His voice. The opening of our spirits to walk in worship teaches us to fear the Lord and walk in humility. This leads us to a lifestyle of developing obedience and holiness that grows from the hunger to abide in Him.

In Romans 12, Paul described worship as the daily sacrifice of our lives and rights to Abba in conformation to His image, as opposed to conformation to the world's ways. He encourages us to present our bodies as a holy, living sacrifice. This, of course, is our act of worship. It's a dangerous thing to court a prophetic spirit while pandering to the desires of the flesh and the world. Worship is our giving Him our all in every area, including our time, our energy, and our money. As worship brings us close to His heart, we open our lives in intimacy, and nothing He asks is too much. One of the ancients, Father Ippolito Durazzo, proclaimed, "However much God costs, the price is never too high."[3]

The knowledge of His love and affection moves us in worship to long for fellowship with Him, and in that place we grow in hearing His voice. David said, "The secret of the Lord is with those who fear Him, and He will show them His covenant" (Ps. 25:14). Indeed, God shares His secrets with those who love Him.

FASTING

In the Sermon on the Mount, Jesus didn't say, "If you fast." He said, "When you fast" (Matt. 6:16). Kings fasted, queens fasted, prophets fasted, servants fasted, Jesus fasted, and the disciples fasted. The biblical precedent has definitely been set. We usually reserve fasting for the extreme circumstances, like someone being about to die or extraordinary spiritual warfare. For the NT church, however, fasting was a regular practice.

There are a lot of good, biblical reasons to fast. We can fast for breakthrough in our lives, churches, ministries, governments, and the nation of Israel (see Esther 4:16). We can fast for the harvest God wants to release in the earth (see John 4:31-35). We can fast over issues of justice and mercy (see Isa. 58). Daniel fasted to receive a breakthrough in revelation (see Dan. 9:3). And though all of these are good, solid reasons for fasting, for our purposes here, however, I am only going to touch the subject as it relates to growing in intimacy and the prophetic.

First, fasting has a way of expanding our hearts to receive more of Him and grow in intimacy. Matthew 6:16-18 elucidates this thought. It reads:

> When you fast, do not look somber as the hypocrites do, for they disfigure their faces to show others they are fasting. Truly I tell you, they have received their reward in full. But when you fast, put oil on your head and wash your face, so that it will not be obvious to others that you are fasting, but only to your Father, who is unseen; and your Father, who sees what is done in secret, will reward you (NIV).

The *secret place* is a phrase that is symbolic of being before the Lord in prayer. Fasting in this regard is an act of love and sacrifice between us and Abba that says, "I know I don't have to do this, but I want my heart capacity to be expanded to receive more of You. Because of that, I'm going to deny myself the pleasure of food to seek Your face." It's the heart cry of the Bride for the presence and friendship of the Bridegroom. It's another expression of the pouring out of our perfume on His feet as an act of love. It's not about earning something. Fasting doesn't make God "owe" me something. Rather, it's about positioning my heart to receive more.

Grace is the unmerited favor by which God forgives us and brings us to Himself. Placing my heart in the position to have as much as I can once I come into the Kingdom is favor. I don't just want to live in the Kingdom. I want as much of the King as I can possibly have, to live in and be expressed through me. Fasting as a lifestyle helps keep my heart attuned to His heart and opens me up to Him in this way. So, in this sense, fasting is connected to growing in intimacy. It's a way of saying, "I want more."

The promise Jesus made to His disciples concerning fasting was the Father would reward them openly. This act of worship, when done with a joyful heart, yields a deeper communion with God and tenderness toward God. It opens our hearts to love, our ears to hear, and our eyes to see. It connects our hearts to the Isaiah 61 heart of God—to see captives set free and brought home. We cannot disconnect operating in the prophetic from God's love of souls. Fasting in agreement with God for souls further opens our awareness to hear and prophesy over unbelievers. For me, this is one of the greatest joys in prophesying.

God's heart is for the release of the captive, and fasting is one way that Jesus demonstrated we can come in line with His heart in this area.

GROWING IN FAITHFULNESS

Faithfulness is a major key in cultivating a prophetic lifestyle. I believe faithfulness is one of the most underrated virtues in the Church today. In a time when everyone wants and expects everything yesterday, the idea of steady labor at ministries that are hidden and unglamorous is not widely embraced.

Sometimes, we have a false romantic notion connected to having a prophetic gift. People imagine, if they have this gift, they will wander around continually inspired, and everyone will be in awe of the grandeur of their gift. I always tried to demystify this concept when talking to people who wanted to join IHOP-KC prophecy teams. My recruitment speech went something like this: "If you commit to join a prophecy team you will be expected to show up every week and prophesy over twelve to fifteen strangers during a two-hour period. If you had a great day, you show up. If you had a really bad day, you show up. If you are broke, you show up. If you had a fight with your spouse or kids, you show up. If you are under spiritual attack (is there anyone who isn't?), you show up." This doesn't sound so glamorous and romantic, does it? Team members can't randomly miss their ministry times and stay on a team, and the "I didn't feel led of the Lord to come today" was not an acceptable excuse.

The way we mature in our gift is to be faithful in practicing it. No matter how we feel, whether we are known or unknown, or whether it seems like we are anointed or un-anointed, the gift grows as our character deepens in the place of simply being faithful.

I know people at IHOP who have served on prophetic teams for years. No one knows them. You wouldn't be able to point them out. They are truly nameless and faceless, yet they prophesy with great kindness and great accuracy. This is the result of faithfulness in the practice of their gift and faithfulness in staying before the Lord as His friend. Jesus so values faithfulness in His Bride,

He is actually known in Revelation as the One who is faithful and true (see Rev. 3:14; 19:11).

There are two aspects to growing in faithfulness in connection with the prophetic. First is the development of faithfulness in the secret place. This is where we get the oil Jesus spoke of in Matthew 25. It's the steady practice of all I have previously addressed in this section, the regular practice of praying Scripture, gazing on the beauty and wonder of Jesus, and pursuing Him in fasting and prayer. It isn't always glamorous, and every day isn't filled with dynamic encounters—though it's nice when they are sprinkled in! It's not about pursuing these things so we can become prophetic; rather, we are pursuing friendship. Growth in the prophetic is a by-product of this. Staying faithful in these key areas will keep the fire of God burning on the altar of our hearts from now until the time He returns or the time we go to be with Him.

At the end of the day, it isn't the church or a ministry or a gift that will keep us in love with Jesus. It's deep friendship that develops over time as we are faithful to stay before Him.

The second aspect of faithfulness has to do with the stewardship we have been given. In Matthew 25:21, Jesus spoke of the good and faithful servant, and in Galatians 6:9-10 Paul encouraged the saints not to be weary in doing good. He, too, encouraged our being faithful.

One of the questions I am asked most frequently regarding how to grow in the prophetic is, "What can I do to develop my gifting?"

The answer is simple—"Prophesy." I don't mean that we should take the gift lightly, but I do mean that we need to regularly place ourselves in the position to prophesy by asking God what He is doing around us in different situations. If we don't prophesy, we won't grow in the gift. We need to learn to ask in church settings, in restaurants, in markets, in homes, or anywhere else we may be. It means we learn to love people by prophesying strength, edification, and encouragement to them in whatever form or arena the Lord gives us to prophesy.

Faithfulness in gifting means that we steward our gifts, not by making them our identity, but by lovingly endeavoring to minister to others as He gives us words. If we ask for more and exercise our faith in using the gift, He will give us more.

FRIENDSHIP FOR THE JOURNEY

A prophetic spirit isn't developed overnight. It's cultivated over a lifetime. At the heart of the journey is the quest for ever-increasing friendship with God. This has been the sustaining power in the lives of the biblical saints. They weren't encountered by doctrines or sermons or duties. They were encountered by the *Living God*, and in that their lives and destinies were radically changed. These encounters were the door to an ongoing friendship in which the wonder of God played a major part.

In praying through the Psalms, not only have I been fascinated with the beauty and ways of God, I have also became fascinated with the amount of revelation David received in his pursuit of God. David had revelation of Jesus as Savior, Jesus as the coming King, the Person of the Holy Spirit, end-time scenarios, and the kinds of things that made glad and moved the heart of God. He was a man who delved into the Person of God with great passion. Perhaps this is why, in spite of his weaknesses, God called him a man after His own heart. He was a true friend of God.

One day while praying in Psalms, I was encountering the goodness and wisdom of God in a very tender and sweet way. I just couldn't help myself. I asked the Lord, "Lord, how come David got so much revelation of You?"

He whispered back to me, "In David's day, there were but a few men who wholeheartedly sought My face. David was one of them, and it was My pleasure to overwhelm him with revelation."

I immediately responded, "Lord, sign me up! I want to be on that list."

It's the wonder of and friendship with God that allows our faith to move past our heads and into our hearts.

Jesus spent three years with the disciples preparing them to carry on the Kingdom after He left. Toward the end, a transformation began taking place within them, and He began to bring them more deeply into His heart. This is reflected in the following verses:

> *Greater love has no one than this: to lay down one's life for one's friends. You are my friends if you do what I command. I no longer call you servants, because a servant does not know his master's business. Instead, I have called you friends, for everything that I learned from my Father I have made known to you. You did not choose me, but I chose you and appointed you so that you might go and bear fruit—fruit that will last—and so that whatever you ask in my name the Father will give you* (John 15:13-16 NIV).

The disciples, for the most part, were a pretty ragtag, self-centered, weak bunch. (There is hope for us!) When Jesus fed the five thousand, the disciples worried about not having enough bread. Jesus walked on the water, then they worried they would drown in a storm. They tried to keep the children from Him, and He said the Kingdom belonged to "such as these." He tried to prepare them for His death, and they argued about who would be the greatest among them. He loved them faithfully and completely all the way to the end. Not because He needed highly talented and gifted men. Not because their natural skills and abilities would lend themselves to usefulness in what Jesus had in mind for them. He loved them because of the value he saw in them, and in the end they became His friends. He saw in them what few others did.

No one would have pegged them to have the courage of a martyr. His love transformed them, and in the three years they spent with Him they became the friends of the Messiah. The point in all this is that He isn't looking for more talented ministers, more educated preachers, and more prophetically endued lay people. He is looking for friends.

John the Baptist is a good example of this. Though he didn't spend great amounts of time with Jesus, he knew Him as friend and called himself *a friend of the Bridegroom*. When Jesus's ministry was increasing and John's was beginning to wind down, he told his disciples, "He must increase, but I must decrease." He wasn't building his own platform or ministry. His joy was fulfilled in seeing his friend Jesus receive the love of the Bride. Jesus described him as the greatest of prophets (see John 3:27-30).

Another example of friendship was Mary Magdalene. When Jesus delivered and saved her, He told her, "Woman, go in peace, your faith has saved you." She took the peace, she took the salvation, but she wouldn't go away (see Luke 7:48-50). She spent the rest of her life seeking to live in the range of His gaze. I can picture her in the midst of the teaching times with Jesus and the disciples as they traveled from place to place, being almost invisible in their midst, yet always caring for Jesus. "Do You need water, Master? Jesus, is there anything You need?"

Her goal in life was just to be with Him. She was near the cross when they crucified Him. She was at the tomb when they buried Him, and she was at the tomb when He was raised (see Matt. 27:56,61; 28:1-7). Her life was all about knowing, loving, and serving Him. I like to imagine that, while Jesus was teaching the Sermon on the Mount to the thousands who were there to hear Him, He felt the burn of one intense gaze from someone in the crowd. He would look, and there would be Mary, lost in His love and His words. No one would have noticed, but I like to think He might have given her a slight nod or a faint smile. Of course, at that, I'm sure Mary's heart would melt. "He loves me!" She could live for weeks on just that one little nod because sitting under His gaze was the desire of her heart.

Perhaps the greatest example of friendship is seen between Jesus and John the apostle. When we first meet John, we discover a young man with great zeal but little understanding. He is ready to call down fire and brimstone on Samaria because they won't receive Jesus; thus he and his brother James got the label *sons of thunder* (see Luke 9:54). There was a hunger and a tenderness that grew up in John, which Jesus saw and nurtured. He would often take Peter and James and John with Him on special missions (see Matt. 17:1). John eventually referred to himself as *the disciple whom Jesus loved*. One of Jesus's last acts on the cross was to give John the responsibility of caring for His own mother (see John 19:25-27). And when it came time for God to release His greatest prophetic revelation of the things regarding the end of the age, who did He choose to give it to? He gave it to His friend John.

In all three of these examples, you will notice that their place with Jesus wasn't based on ministry or place or position. These things were gladly laid down. They fell in love with the Man who delivered them. They fell in love with the Beautiful One who laid down His life for His friends. To each of them, He was worthy of everything they had to give.

Many Christians come into the Kingdom madly in love with Jesus, but slowly that love for Him gets replaced or diluted by church duties or ministries or other responsibilities. After forty years of following Jesus and being in ministry, I have seen a lot of people burn out. The cause almost always can be traced to the place where first love and friendship got replaced with ministry, duty, place, or lost fascination. For this reason, developing an ever-deepening love for friendship with Jesus will always be the key in growing in a prophetic lifestyle. It's both the desired experience and the goal of our lives. It's all about that long journey into friendship with God. Out of that relationship, the prophetic can flourish. As I already mentioned, He shares His secrets with His friends.

GETTING PLUGGED IN

1. Which of the aspects mentioned in this chapter struck your heart the most? Why? How would you explain your revelation to another person?

2. What are three things you can start doing today to begin or increase your pursuit of friendship with God in your journey?

3. Make a simple plan to increase the expression of your prophetic gift in the arenas of your life. Ask the Holy Spirit to help you put it into action for the increase of your faithful stewardship of your gift.

NOTES

1. St. Francis de Sales, *Treatise on the Love of God* (Rockford, Illinois: TAN Books and Publishers, 2009) 21.

2. Wayne Grudem, *The Gift of Prophecy in the New Testament and Today* (Wheaton, Illinois: Crossway, 2000) 103.

3. Alphonso Ligouri, *The Practice of the Love of Jesus Christ (A Liguori Classic)* (Liguori, Missouri: Liguori Publications, 1997) 51.

THE PROPHETIC MINISTER AS SERVANT

THERE ARE MANY DEFINITIONS FOR WHAT PROPHECY IS. EDIFYING the Church, encouraging the saints, and speaking God's Word over circumstances and situations are a few I have heard. My favorite is simple. *It's washing the feet of the saints with the Word of the Lord.* I like this definition because it lines up with the testimony of Jesus in that He came to serve, not be served, and this demonstrates that prophesying is a servant act, done not primarily for the prophesier's benefit, but rather for the receiver's benefit.

I love to prophesy. The joy and exhilaration of hearing from God for an individual, and then giving a word that brings instant encouragement and clarity and wisdom for a season down the road, is greatly satisfying. The practice and experience of prophesying has taught me personal lessons about faith, humility, compassion, and grace. I have been touched by deeper elements of the heart of God, how He sees people and feels about people, how He heals through words of love, and the crazy mysteries that He reveals through simple prophetic words. I love and enjoy all of these aspects of prophetic ministry. Yet, at the end of the day, as much as I enjoy the gift, it really isn't about me. It's about the body of Christ.

At the Last Supper, Jesus took a good deal of time to lovingly wash the disciples' feet. We can miss much of what this encounter must have looked like if we skim over it. This was personal to Jesus. While He was making a corporate point and setting a corporate example, He loved these men, even Judas Iscariot. Though it's not recorded in the Scripture, I imagine that Jesus didn't just wash their feet, but rather took time with each one to encourage him, bless him, and possibly even to leave each with a personal prophetic word. He knew what was coming and He wanted them to be prepared for His crucifixion and to also have an experiential picture engrained on their hearts for the Church, which would soon be born.

So here we have the picture of the eternal Lamb, slain from the foundations of the earth, the Son of God who eternally existed with His Father, who had all power and authority, stooping down to wash the feet of men. Other than the cross, I cannot think of a greater physical act of servanthood demonstrated by Jesus. After He finished ministering to each of the disciples, He made the corporate point.

> *When he had finished washing their feet, he put on his clothes and returned to his place. "Do you understand what I have done for you?" he asked them. "You call me 'Teacher' and 'Lord,' and rightly so, for that is what I am. Now that I, your Lord and Teacher, have washed your feet, you also should wash one another's feet. I have set you an example that you should do as I have done for you" (John 13:12-15 NIV).*

Here, Jesus literally washes the feet of His disciples with His love and His words. This brings me back to that simple definition of a prophetic word—*washing the feet of the saints with the word of the Lord.* We can immensely enjoy the gift of prophecy, but we are to function in it as servants of the Church.

The phrase, "My servants the prophets," is used nineteen times in the Bible. God chose men and women whose hearts were knit to His heart to impart His word to. Those who would serve Jesus's Bride in the gift of prophecy must be servant-hearted in their administration of the gift. We are friends of the Bridegroom but also servants of the Bride.

In this section, I will explore the gift of prophecy from the perspective of building the Church with a servant heart. I want to touch on First Corinthians 12, 13, and 14. In exploring this subject. I will only skim the surface of these chapters, simply focusing on the underlying emphasis that spiritual gifts are to be used in the context of serving the Church. The blessing and benefit to those who function in the gift is secondary to this purpose.

Chapter Eight

FIRST CORINTHIANS 12

ONE OF PAUL'S MAIN POINTS IN THIS CHAPTER IS THAT THE MANI-
festation of a gift to an individual is given not primarily for that
person, but rather for the edification of the whole body. He says
gifts are "given to each one for the profit of all" (1 Cor. 12:7). While
there is great joy in ministering and growing in a gift, we must
realize that God has gifted us to help, encourage, and strengthen
the Church.

I love the gift of prophecy. I enjoy moving in it, and I enjoy
seeing the results when it's done right. One day I was ministering
to someone in the IHOP-KC prophecy rooms, and as I was sharing
the whispers of the Lord, Jesus snuck in a phrase that was just for
me. He whispered, "I love it when you prophesy."

I was shocked, and I almost said it out loud to the person I
was prophesying to. I never thought about the joy God took in me
while I was enjoying Him by ministering in the prophetic. It was
the kiss of His encouragement to go even deeper in the gift. Yet,
as much as I enjoy the gift, I know that primarily it's given to build

the Church. The fact that I get to prophesy is secondary to that truth and purpose.

For many, the only example they see of the prophetic is at conferences when prophetic ministry is expressed from the stage or the platform. They see the glory of it, so to speak, and then desire to take the gift, have the stage, and move in power. They see the glamor, influence, and ministry of the prophetic and make it their goal to get there. The truth is, few will ever really have that platform, and for those who do, it will come with a price. The gift of prophecy isn't given for that reason. It's not meant to be a stepping stone or a mark of personal maturity. It's meant to build the Church.

Prophetic servants are gifts to build the body in love. They are given so Joe the Plumber can strengthen and edify John the Carpenter at church or on the job or in Wal-Mart. They are given so the manifestations of God can be released to encourage the Church and win the lost on a local level. Average, weak people who love God and are trying to grow forward are equipped with gifts, not to show off their spirituality, but to build their churches and win their communities for Jesus. Once we understand and embrace this, there is actually great freedom for us. We get to be ourselves, serving from where God has placed us, out of what He has put in our hearts, and without having to prophesy like the guy on the platform or someone else we saw.

In line with this thought, we understand that gifts are given to build the whole Church, not to establish an elite corps. One of the things I have seen at times in the expression of the prophetic among some is the concept of being the group *on the cutting edge*. There is a subtle air of pride that can easily slip in, leading to the notion that prophetic people are more spiritually mature and are part of the "in crowd," thus deserving more honor. This can lead to critical attitudes and divisiveness. We advertise the strength of our gift in the hope that we will be honored because of it, but God honors those who are weak and in need. Paul illustrates this point in First Corinthians 12:24-26. He says:

But God composed the body, having given greater honor to that part which lacks it, that there should be no schism in the body, but that the members should have the same care for one another. And if one member suffers, all the members suffer with it; or if one member is honored, all the members rejoice with it.

God delights in honoring and celebrating the whole Bride, especially those who are weak or seem to have less than others. The purpose of the prophetic gift in this context is to call out and honor the weak, to encourage and strengthen them. One of the main functions of the gift of prophecy, then, is to serve as an encouraging blanket over the Bride—one that covers, not exposes; that honors, not humiliates; that celebrates, not disgraces. There is no room for elitism in this ministry, but rather, along with other callings and ministries in the local church, we build the entire Church up in love. Even the highest offices in the Church are given as gifts to serve the entire body, not as governmental places from which policy and privilege are doled out from ivory towers. No, Paul says in verse 28, "And God has appointed these in the church: first apostles, second prophets, third teachers, after that miracles, then gifts of healings, helps, administrations, varieties of tongues."

This is not meant to be a comprehensive list. The point is that even the roles of apostle, prophet, and teacher are to be administered from the place of love and service. Apostles may be first in government, but they are also to be first in service. In his book, *The Gift of Prophecy in the New Testament and Today*, Wayne Grudem points out that even with the five-fold ministry callings, greatness is measured not by authority but by usefulness to the Church.[1]

Too often people seek these positions for their influence and prestige without giving thought to the cost and servanthood factors these positions require. There is a certain romanticism in the Church about these offices that has not considered the call and the cost. A quick glance at First Corinthians 4:9-13 should be enough to redefine this romance, especially these verses:

> To this very hour we go hungry and thirsty, we are in rags, we are brutally treated, we are homeless. We work hard with our own hands. When we are cursed, we bless; when we are persecuted, we endure it; when we are slandered, we answer kindly. We have become the scum of the earth, the garbage of the world—right up to this moment (1 Corinthians 4:11-13 NIV).

I have had people introduce themselves to me as apostles and prophets. I wholeheartedly believe in and embrace the five-fold ministry as expressed in Ephesians 4. I truly believe God is raising up apostles and prophets in this hour, along with pastors and teachers and evangelists. But when I see the lack of humility and spiritual weight of some who take on the titles, I want to ask them to pull up their shirts and show me their stripes! Very few biblical apostles and prophets escaped life without some form of persecution or suffering.

At the end of the day, Jesus won't be looking for how important or famous we were as much as the methods and motives with which we served His Bride. If He washed the feet of the disciples in love, will He expect any less from us in the expression of our gifts and callings?

Now, we are unashamedly commanded to desire the best gifts. This sounds a little selfish, but there is a reason to desire the best gifts. The best gifts are those that do the most to edify, strengthen, and build up the body. They are gifts that lead the Bride to maturity and the full expression of the love and power of Christ in her witness. The more people are functioning in these best gifts, the more the body is edified. When Moses said that he wished for all God's people to be prophets, I believe he had this thought in mind (see Num. 11:29). Still, even the best gifts, the ones to be most desired, are to be desired so we can serve in greater measure. This stands in contrast to the way some would view these gifts.

Some church leaders and pastors favor or put on pedestals those with such gifts as prophecy or healing. Sometimes, this is done with sincerity, but then there are times it's done to increase the draw and the popularity of their churches. This can make those with these gifts feel more special or give them a sense of being elite. If their security is not deeply rooted in their identity in God, they may face great temptation, and their lives can be destroyed.

In truth, God gives these gifts so the body can be better served, not for the exaltation of an individual or a church ministry. While we are commanded to pursue the best gifts, we are also commanded to operate in them through the supremacy of love. Paul says, "But earnestly desire the best gifts. And yet I show you a more excellent way" (1 Cor. 12:31).

GETTING PLUGGED IN

1. Why do you think Paul named prophecy as the best gift?

2. My emphasis in this chapter was that the gifts are to be used to serve the body. If we are not fully sure of our hearts being in the right place, should we refrain from using our gifts? Why or why not?

3. What are some things we can do to resist temptations to pride or elitism while continuing to grow in the expression of our gifts?

NOTE

1. Wayne Grudem, *The Gift of Prophecy in the New Testament and Today* (Wheaton, Illinois: Crossway, 2000) 53.

Chapter Nine

FIRST CORINTHIANS 13

Paul concluded First Corinthians 12 by introducing the context spiritual gifts are to flow through in chapter 13. I'm going to highlight the points that strongly relate to attitudes and expressions of prophetic ministry. This chapter emphasizes our personal pursuit of the way of love in the administration of gifts of the Spirit.

I want to use First Corinthians 13:11 as a starting place for this section. It reads, "When I was a child, I spoke as a child, I understood as a child, I thought as a child; but when I became a man, I put away childish things."

Those who are gifted prophetically should seek to mature in both their gift and their character. The gift of prophecy isn't given based on maturity of years in the faith or personal merit. It's given to build the body, and the mature, as well as the immature, may receive the gift.

Love calls us to grow beyond childishness and immaturity into fruitful servants in both character and expression. There are things a two-year-old does that some might consider cute, but the same things are not so cute when the two-year-old turns twenty. Paul is encouraging the Church to mature in gifting and in character. A strong biblical and spiritual foundation is vital for believers to grow up in Christ. If our prophetic words are going to increase in weight and anointing, then we must aim at transitioning from giving prophetic messages to becoming prophetic messengers. This is no quick and easy journey. It takes time, diligence, perseverance, and a continuing hunger to live out of God's heart.

For those who want to quickly rise to the top, this can seem painstakingly slow. I'm not saying that God can't release highly accurate information to immature vessels. I think we have all seen or experienced that. I'm saying that, for our sakes and the sakes of those we minister to, God's way is to establish a strong foundation on which to release greater power and anointing. We all start at the childish stage. No one skips straight to maturity. The point isn't that we are childish early on in our faith. It's that we make it our goal not to stay there. The goal is Christlikeness. A childish minister can fall into James's description of pride and immaturity, taking the view that the gift and its function are all about him and his agenda and recognition. James says in his epistle:

> Who is wise and understanding among you? Let them show it by their good life, by deeds done in the humility that comes from wisdom. But if you harbor bitter envy and selfish ambition in your hearts, do not boast about it or deny the truth. Such "wisdom" does not come down from heaven but is earthly, unspiritual, demonic. For where you have envy and selfish ambition, there you find disorder and every evil practice (James 3:13-16 NIV).

We must seek to mature and minister out of love, which has at its heart the welfare of others. In this light, love must be the foundation and motivation for all ministry expression. Paul does a masterful job of conveying this truth in the thirteenth chapter of First Corinthians. He says:

> *Though I speak with the tongues of men and of angels, but have not love, I have become sounding brass or a clanging cymbal. And though I have the gift of prophecy, and understand all mysteries and all knowledge, and though I have all faith, so that I could remove mountains, but have not love, I am nothing. And though I bestow all my goods to feed the poor, and though I give my body to be burned, but have not love, it profits me nothing* (1 Corinthians 13:1-3).

Love requires intimacy, and intimacy requires sacrifice (though to one in love, acts of sacrifice are never defined as duty). Love calls us to lay our lives down for Him. This is expressed through our gifts and ministry to Him and the body of Christ. On the last day, He will tell some, "Depart from Me. I never knew you," though they will claim to have done mighty miracles (see Matt. 7:23). "I never knew you" indicates that they did their "stuff" outside of the place of love and servanthood. In other words, there was no intimacy. So their miracles were done to exalt their own names and their own ministries, and these ministries won't stand the test of Christ's fire at the judgment.

You may be able to minister without loving, but you can't love without ministering. This is because love looks beyond what benefits us exclusively. The expression of true love will be revealed in serving others without regard to how they can bless us or what they can do for us. I have heard it said that one measure of a man's love is revealed in how he treats those who can do him no good. Jesus expressed the ultimate definition of love when He said, "Greater love has no one than this, than to lay down one's life for his friends" (John 15:13).

In this light, key characteristics prophetic servants should seek to grow in are kindness, meekness, and humility. So Paul gives us the following advice:

> *Love suffers long and is kind; love does not envy; love does not parade itself, is not puffed up; does not behave rudely, does not seek its own, is not provoked, thinks no evil; does not rejoice in iniquity, but rejoices in the truth; bears all things, believes all things, hopes all things, endures all things* (1 Corinthians 13:4-7).

Love is the heart of servant ministry, and its cloak is humility, kindness, faith, and encouragement.

I was teaching a prophetic seminar to some of our IHOP-KC interns when one of them gave me a scenario and asked me to respond to it. The student had been in a church where there were a few prophetic people. The behavior of one of them was somewhat rude and brash. When the student asked a leader about it, the behavior was excused because the person was prophetic. The idea was that this was an eccentric prophetic characteristic and, therefore, above judgment. I have seen the same thing before in different churches and have known prophetic people who could get away with unkind behavior that others couldn't because it was part of the so-called *prophetic personality package.*

But John wrote in Revelation 19:10 that the testimony of Jesus is the spirit of prophecy. Paul isn't just describing types of love in this chapter. He is describing the character of the Man, Jesus Christ, who Himself is the Spirit of prophecy. He is our standard of behavior, and He knew nothing of rudeness and pride.

> *Let this mind be in you which was also in Christ Jesus, who, being in the form of God, did not consider it robbery to be equal with God, but made Himself of no reputation, taking the form of a bondservant, and coming in the likeness of men. And being found in appearance as*

*a man, He humbled Himself and became obedient to
the point of death, even the death of the cross. Therefore God also has highly exalted Him and given Him the
name which is above every name, that at the name of
Jesus every knee should bow, of those in heaven, and of
those on earth, and of those under the earth, and that
every tongue should confess that Jesus Christ is Lord, to
the glory of God the Father* (Philippians 2:5-11).

If the heart of the NT gift of prophecy is to strengthen, edify,
and encourage the body, then the conduct of those seeking to grow
in this gift should be lining up with the purpose of the gift itself,
which is to serve the body.

Paul also said that love does not parade itself and it isn't puffed
up, meaning that love doesn't brag, put on a show, or draw attention to its own works. Love moves in humility and meekness.

I was once asked by a student, "How do I learn to grow in
humility regarding the prophetic?"

My answer was, "Don't worry. You will have many opportunities in life to have your question answered!"

One of the greatest enemies of the prophetic is pride. Think
about it a moment. As you grow in the prophetic, you hear God's
voice for other people in ways that they know you know the secrets
of their hearts. Sometimes, you know about their prayers, their circumstances, their families, things they journal, etc. Some think
you see all these things about everyone all the time. When people have this perception, two things can happen. First, you get the
reputation for being a prophetic person; some will even call you
a prophet. Second, the demand on you to minister will increase.
These two things by themselves are enough to spark pride in the
most humble of the humble.

We must keep our hearts rooted in humility. I like to remember a saying I once heard, "Your halo only has to slip six inches to
become a noose." It is better to go low and stay low, not letting the

greatest things people say about us or the worst things people say about us be the measure of our emotional state. We will face the temptation of pride, and unless we are rooted in humility and intimacy with His heart, we will fail miserably. The wonderful thing about God is that He doesn't give us an *F* on these tests when we mess up. He just keeps letting us take them until we pass!

God is raising up a faceless, nameless generation whose hearts and joy are the exaltation of Jesus. This doesn't mean we are to act humble about our gifts and calling; it just means that, at the end of the day, we want to be known as obedient lovers of God first and anointed ministers second. We want to be humble! We want the attitude of John Baptist who said:

> *He who has the bride is the bridegroom; but the friend of the bridegroom, who stands and hears him, rejoices greatly because of the bridegroom's voice. Therefore this joy of mine is fulfilled. He must increase, but I must decrease* (John 3:29-30).

The joy of prophesying is mostly fulfilled in seeing how a good prophetic word makes people love Jesus more.

Another characteristic a prophetic servant must continue to grow in is teachableness. We must be open to both teaching and correction because love rejoices in the truth.

I have known some who have taken on the attitude that they hear from God and they don't need any help or input from anyone else. They put themselves in the position of becoming their own standard, thus closing themselves off from learning from their mistakes or receiving correction in any form from someone else. If we are going to grow in the gift of prophecy, we will have to take risks at times. To open our mouths and prophesy is a great step of faith, and there will be times that we miss it and get it wrong. In such cases, as I've said before, we must not spiritualize our mistakes and explain them away. We must be teachable and accountable for what we say. If I prophesy wrongly over someone, I want to know about it. As you know, I learned early on that to grow, I must be accountable. In whatever way teaching or correction comes, we must learn to be receptive and accountable in regard to what, how, and why we prophesy.

The heart of the prophetic servant is to be rooted and grounded in truth and righteousness. Yet love "bears all things, believes all things, hopes all things, endures all things" (1 Cor. 13:7). You see, the prophetic servant believes the best without looking for darkness and the pronouncement of judgment on those he is ministering to. When such things are present, the heart of the prophetic servant isn't to condemn, but rather to redeem.

John chapter 21 expounds well on this thought. Jesus joined the disciples on the beach for breakfast. Peter was saved and was glad to be there with the risen Lord, but he may have felt disqualified to continue in his place as an apostle because of his denial of the Lord. Through a series of questions Jesus restored Peter back into his place, and He did it by reminding him of the prophetic promises that He Himself had spoken over him.

Three times Jesus asked him, "Do you love Me?" With each of Peter's responses, Jesus brought him back to His prophetic promises. Jesus's command for Peter to feed His lambs took Peter back to the prophetic promise Jesus gave him in the boat when they were fishing together, "Don't be afraid; I will make you a fisher of men" (see Luke 5:10). He was reminding him that the promise still remained, that he would bring the lambs (unbelievers to new believers) into the Kingdom and feed them (see John 21:15).

After Peter's reply to His second question, Jesus called Peter to tend His sheep. This was Jesus reminding Peter that He prophesied he would be a rock on whom He could build His church (see Matt. 16:17-19). The promise remained for him to tend His sheep and pastor the flock of God.

Jesus's third question and response went to the heart of Peter's brokenness and failure. Peter promised Jesus that he would go to jail for Him and even die for Him. He miserably failed in that assignment, denying Jesus three times. Jesus's response indicated to Peter that he would get the chance again, and this time he would pass the test (see John 21:18-19). We know he did when, at his own crucifixion, Peter requested to be crucified upside down, not feeling worthy to die like Jesus died.

Peter had been defining and disqualifying himself by his failure, but Jesus would have none of it. By reminding Peter of his prophetic promises and who He saw him to be, He prophesied Peter out of his failure and into his calling. He was bringing Peter restoration by giving him heaven's picture of who he was and what his destiny was. Jesus's love for Peter was manifest through His believing in Peter as a man, releasing hope to his heart, and enduring his failure in love.

Honestly, I know my own sins and weaknesses. I don't need someone else to prophesy them to me. I need someone to prophesy me out of them. When I know by the Spirit that someone is in sin, my first question to God is, "Who is this person to You, and what are they for?" I want to know God's plan for them and how He sees them. That is what I will prophesy, along with the encouragement to enter the season of sanctification so they can receive all He has for them. This way, whether in a prophecy room or public context, no one but the individual knows their sin has been identified. They can repent, but even more, they have reason to do so because now they have hope about the Father's love toward them and His commitment to bring them into their calling.

This doesn't mean that there aren't times when we might have to expose sin and bring a hard word. But this must be done according to biblical protocol (see Matt. 18:15-20), with great tenderness, and with the desire for the redemption of the person as the key goal. It should be painful to the prophetic servant to have to deal with such a situation. Some think it's their gift to uncover sin and expose people's weaknesses. If it makes us feel good to prophesy judgment over individuals or places, then we need to examine our hearts.

After forty years of calling Judah back to God and prophesying His desire to show mercy in the midst of judgment, Jeremiah took no joy in the day he saw Jerusalem destroyed and its surviving captives marched out of the city in chains. He wept. Lamentations is the testimony of the heart of a prophet feeling the weight and burden of the Lord in response to judgment. So the heart of the prophetic servant should be to rejoice in truth, believing, hoping, and bearing all things for the body, looking for the best and calling forth repentance, redemption, and restoration when weakness or sin is exposed.

Wayne Grudem has given a good, practical expression for how prophets can move in love. They can demonstrate patience by waiting their turn to prophesy, not being rude (see 1 Cor. 13:5; 14:31). They aim at speaking to others for their benefit and encouragement (see 1 Cor. 13:5; 14:3). They learn to submit words for evaluation, demonstrating teachableness (see 1 Cor. 13:4; 14:29). They demonstrate meekness by giving way to others to prophesy (see 1 Cor. 13:4-5; 14:30). Finally, if they have to expose sin, they will do so for redemptive purposes and in kindness (see 1 Cor. 13:5-6; 14:24-25).[1]

I used to approach this chapter from the perspective of breaking down the description of love, characteristic by characteristic, focusing on every individual attribute listed. While this was helpful, eventually I realized that all these characteristics are present in a Man—the Man Christ Jesus. If we wholeheartedly pursue intimacy with Him, these characteristics will find their way into our lives. As they do, they will spill into every area, including our prophetic ministries.

GETTING PLUGGED IN

1. How does God use our spiritual gifts to test and refine our own hearts?

2. Should a person's high level of operation in a spiritual gift excuse him or her from being accountable for behavior that is not Christlike?

3. First Corinthians 13:5-7 describes love as believing, bearing, hoping, and enduring all things. What does this have to do with prophetic ministry?

4. Ask the Lord to show you anything in your life that doesn't function from the motivation of love. Don't do your own digging. Rather, let the Holy Spirit show you. Commit those things to the Lord, and ask Him to bring transformation.

NOTE

1. Grudem, *The Gift of Prophecy*, 131.

Chapter Ten

FIRST CORINTHIANS 14

PART OF THE PURPOSE OF PAUL'S INSTRUCTION IN THIS CHAPTER was to address the Corinthians' overemphasis on the gift of tongues. Many were caught up in ecstatic experiences in tongues, and that activity was taking precedence over the need for corporate edification. Paul was not taking away from the value of tongues; rather, he was emphasizing the corporate good over the individual good in the corporate gathering of the Church.

THE EDIFICATION OF THE BODY

Paul's theme in addressing this is consistent with his instruction in chapters 12 and 13, with the main point being that the body is to serve one another in love and the outflow of that should be common edification. Paul expresses that thought in verse 20, where he says, "Brethren, do not be children in understanding; however, in malice be babes, but in understanding be mature."

To build up the body, Paul encourages gifts like prophecy, teaching, and tongues with interpretation as key expressions in the corporate gatherings. He challenges them to seek prophecy as the most edifying of the gifts.

> *Pursue love, and desire spiritual gifts, but especially that you may prophesy. ...He who prophesies speaks edification and exhortation and comfort to men...he who prophesies edifies the church. ...Brethren, do not be children in understanding; however, in malice be babes, but in understanding be mature* (1 Corinthians 14:1,3-4,20).

Paul is again emphasizing that gifts are given to edify the Church, not just bless the individual who is moving in the gift. The corporate gathering doesn't exist simply to focus on one person's gift. It's about the encouragement of the saints. Church, we need to grow up in this just as Paul challenges us to do and come to church with the attitude of giving, honoring, and blessing more than receiving and wanting to be recognized for our positions. There are eight admonishments to the church in this chapter to administrate gifts and service in the ways that most edify and encourage the *corporate* body (see 1 Cor. 14:3-5,12,19,26,31,40). That is to focus of the gifts of the Spirit, including prophecy.

The question the prophetic servant asks isn't, "When do I get to release my gift?" Rather, it should be, "When and how can I use my gifts to best build up and edify the Church?" It takes us back to Paul's admonition in chapter 13 to set aside childish things and move on to maturity.

CHARACTERISTICS OF THE PROPHETIC SERVANT

In the context of seeking to flow in gifts that build the body, Paul continues to encourage humility, love, and meekness in the corporate expression of those gifts.

Let two or three prophets speak, and let the others judge. But if anything is revealed to another who sits by, let the first keep silent. For you can all prophesy one by one, that all may learn and all may be encouraged. And the spirits of the prophets are subject to the prophets. For God is not the author of confusion but of peace, as in all the churches of the saints. ...Therefore, brethren, desire earnestly to prophesy, and do not forbid to speak with tongues. Let all things be done decently and in order (1 Corinthians 14:29-33;39-40).

Paul was calling those who were recognized as prophets (I'm arbitrarily applying this to those who are highly gifted as well) to demonstrate corporate unity and meekness in the expression of their gifts. The expression of prophecy in harmony among the prophets would both encourage and teach the body.

There are three characteristics that are required of prophetic servants in the fulfilling of the instruction Paul gives here. The first is a humble, teachable spirit. Verse 29 says, "Let two or three prophets speak, and let the others judge." First, the revelation that is being submitted must be allowed to be judged. I have met many "Thus sayeth the Lord" folks who use the phrase as the tag on their word in such a way that you feel, if you judge it, you are questioning God Himself. Leaders and others are made to feel as if they are disagreeing with God if they question the vessel.

Sometimes, when such people disagree with someone about something, instead of saying they disagree and being open to healthy debate or discussion, they say, "I have a check in my spirit about that," implying they have the exclusive track and inroad with the Holy Spirit. How can anyone disagree with or question that?

I served as the leader over our prophecy teams for about a year. We had regular meetings with about twelve strong leaders with diverse views and personalities. We were in a season when we were establishing some foundations, protocols, and values for our teams to grow in. There often was more than one opinion on how something should be done. There were a few occasions when things got tense in the room and the "check in my spirit" card would be played. We eventually agreed the phrase could only be used when it related to something that was spiritually or scripturally wrong or unclean, but could not be used in relation to people in the room in the expression of their ideas. Mature prophetic people must be able to submit their words and not be offended if those words are judged and not given either the weight, or the immediate attention, they feel they deserve.

I like what Grudem says regarding these verses: "The idea is that there were local prophets in local congregations. They themselves were proven (not infallible, but proven in character and gifts). It is not the prophets that were being judged, but their words or messages. This would be done by the congregation and it is supposed, that the leaders would head this up."[1]

In First Thessalonians 5:20-21, Paul echoes what he expresses in this passage in a little different way. He says that we shouldn't despise prophecy, but we should test it and hold fast to parts of the word that are good, indicating that there may be parts we reject or at least give less weight to. As prophetic people, God wants us to be humble in the use of our gifts and teachable regarding the fruit they are bearing.

The second characteristic prophetic people are encouraged to embrace here is meekness—the willingness to defer to others if they are being highlighted or are getting something while we are not. This is seen in his admonition to first keep silent while something is being revealed by another. One of the hardest things for any prophetic person to do is to keep silent! When we have what we think is the breakthrough word, we don't want to wait to give it. We don't want to hear what the other two prophetic vessels have to say. The question that must be answered at the end of the day is not, "Did I get to give my word?" Rather, "Was the body edified through the release of the prophetic word?"

There have been many occasions when I have been in the corporate meeting and have had what I was sure was the word of the Lord, but for whatever reason there wasn't place or time to release it. As I would listen and watch, most of the time that word came forth, either in the worship or very strongly through the preaching of the Word. Instead of being disappointed, I was encouraged, first that I was hearing correctly, and second that the word on God's heart came forth.

There will be times when our gifts seem hidden while others' gifts seem to be highlighted. Most likely God is teaching us to love the low place, knowing that our season will change and the one who is highlighted now will have the same season we are having and we will have the one they are having. I love this quotation by Thomas à Kempis:

> What others say will get a hearing, and what you say will be disparaged. Others will ask for something and get it. You will ask and be refused. Others will be loudly praised by their colleagues, and you will be passed over in silence. This or that assignment will be conferred on others, while you will be judged as good for nothing. The Lord uses such trials to test his faithful servants, to see how they have learned to control themselves and stay calm. At times human nature will protest; but you will profit greatly if you bear it all in silence.[2]

I have seen many come and go through the years. The ones with the staying power don't credit their giftedness for their longevity in their walk and ministry. They credit the faithfulness of God and the grace to find Him in the ups and downs and highs and lows of the different seasons of life and of the human heart. Meekness among prophetic vessels is highly valued by God and will increase edification in the Church not just by their timely words, but also by their godly actions.

I once heard the saying, "Prophets are known on earth by what they say, but they are known in heaven by what they don't say." Perhaps part of that is what Paul has in mind here.

The third characteristic prophetic vessels need to embrace is self-control as "the spirits of the prophets are subject to the prophets." In the context of what Paul is teaching here, this means that we are not under compulsion nor do we have to give our word the instant we receive it. Again, the most important thing is the edification of the body, not the release of our word.

Outside of a few exceptions where we know that we know it is a *now* word, we can wait on God and seek to give our word at the time that will flow with what the Holy Spirit is doing in the meeting and at a time that will release the most edification. And even when we have the *now* word, it still needs to be submitted to the leadership. As we grow in our gifting, there will actually be times when we may get a word for a meeting in advance so we can pray about how God wants to release it and actually talk to leaders before the meeting even starts so it can be released with maximum edification.

If we are growing in learning to fellowship with the Holy Spirit, we understand that we aren't waiting for an anointing to come on us. He is already living in us. He can speak to us anytime, and the word is subject to our will in cooperation with Him as to when to release it. Growing in the characteristic of self-control will not only help us operate in our gifts with more effectiveness, it will also keep us out of a lot of trouble. We can learn to heed the advice of James, "So then, my beloved brethren, let every man be swift to hear, slow to speak" (James 1:19).

When we learn to function in these ways in our meetings, the Church will be edified, and those growing in the prophetic will mature and bear greater fruit. The Church will not only be strengthened by the prophetic words, but also by the example of the prophetic unity that is demonstrated.

There was a reason Paul told the Thessalonians not to despise prophecy. When prophetic vessels are immature and unruly and prophetic words are weak, the Church begins to despise the prophetic. Paul is saying that the answer isn't in throwing the prophetic out the window, but rather to invest in maturing it. This is obviously a work in progress in the Church today.

For things to be done decently and in order, sometimes someone has to give their place to another or submit to someone else with a servant heart. These things often only get worked out through the conflicts that expose what is in our hearts. When we set aside offense and get over ourselves, we know we are on the right track. The question at the end of the day is, "Was the Church strengthened and edified to the maximum the gifts would allow?" If the answer is *yes*, then who gets the credit for that breakthrough word is not so important.

GETTING PLUGGED IN

1. What are the dangers and possible results of comparing our ability in operating in the prophetic with someone else? What can we do to overcome such things?

2. How does unity among the prophetic people in a church edify the whole church?

3. How can an overemphasized focus on our place in prophetic ministry make us vulnerable to our hearts being offended? How can it hinder the church?

NOTES

1   Grudem, *The Gift of Prophecy*, 131.

2.   Alphonso Ligouri, *The Practice of the Love of Jesus Christ* (A Liguori Classic) (Liguori, Missouri: Liguori Publications, 1997) 102.

Chapter Eleven

A FEW FINAL THOUGHTS

THERE IS GREAT JOY IN MOVING IN THE GIFT OF PROPHECY. IT HAS been my joy over the years to train multitudes to function in this gift. The look on the face of the prophesier when they first do it and get it right is always a delight to watch. The realization that God actually speaks to us about other people unto their strength, edification, and encouragement is nothing short of intoxicating. Most people are excited just to do this once. But the prospect of this gift increasing and being a major part of their life and calling is over the top.

My challenge to those wanting to grow in the gift is to consider where they want to be with the gift in one year, three years, and then five years. Viewing the gift of prophecy and the cultivation of a prophetic spirit from the long-range, servant perspective will produce fruit, both immediately and down the road.

Focusing on a life of serving rather than being *the minister* gives priority to building character as opposed to building a place or position as ministers. It keeps us seeking a place at His altar as opposed to building an altar to place.

My gift mix may change during the course of my life. There will be seasons when my gift is in demand and seasons when my gift may be hidden from the ministry perspective. By staying faithful, I am also setting an example for the next generation. My greatest accomplishment in connection with the prophetic may be that one young person who received something from me—who went out and set the world on fire. None but God may know this, but He who sees in secret will reward us at the end of the day.

Lastly, this attitude keeps me focused on the age to come. I understand that I am building on the foundation of gold, silver, and precious stones, establishing a life and a work that will stand the test of the fire, thus producing millennial rewards. Success is measured by simple obedience, not in numbers or who knows our names. This perspective keeps moving us forward as friends of the Bridegroom, serving His Bride with the same zeal with which we serve Him.

GETTING PLUGGED IN

1. In your own experience and observation, what are the three greatest enemies or temptations prophetic people face? How can these things be overcome?

2. What are three things prophetic people can do to help themselves stay encouraged?

3. What are the benefits of long-range thinking about the development of your prophetic gift?

LEADING PROPHETIC PEOPLE

MOST OF THE EMPHASIS IN THIS BOOK HAS BEEN TOWARD DEVEL-oping the prophetic in the local church. In many ways, this task begins and ends with the local church pastor. I have taught many seminars with Catholic, Protestant, conservative, and charismatic pastors present. I have heard the horror stories of prophetic ministry gone wrong, how individuals have been hurt and churches split. Many have become gun-shy regarding opening the door for the development of prophetic people and the flow of prophetic expression in their churches.

However, I am convinced that the prophetic, when used in the right context, not only builds the local church, but actually can make the pastor's job easier. In fact, it can be of great encouragement to the pastor and the entire leadership team.

The key lies in the approach we take to embracing and releasing the prophetic in our churches. I believe that much of the *trouble* that sometimes accompanies prophetic ministry can be avoided if leaders have clarity on the front end of what the prophetic should look like and how it should function on individual and corporate levels. If leaders have clarity on what they are building, it will be easier to encourage, guide, and correct the expression of the prophetic in the church as it grows and unfolds.

Leaders often open the door without a clear idea of how it should look. Many times, it's like jumping into a process that is already happening instead of starting something at the beginning with clear parameters of how it will operate and where it will go. While the *midstream* approach may work initially to encourage the church and the prophetic ones in the midst, it can backfire later when individuals take on more authority than they are equipped to deal with or the church is prepared to give them. Often, the result at this point is that some prophetic people take on a martyr/rejection attitude and leaders shut down the prophetic. If we implement a great deal of prayer and planning on the front end, much of the collateral damage can be eliminated. Obviously, this won't solve all the problems, as people are people and we all bring our weaknesses to the table with us, but those things can be minimized with some vision on the front end.

In this section, I want to briefly touch on a few practical ways to approach a vision for the prophetic as well as discuss some different expressions of the prophetic and give some ideas on training and releasing prophetic ministry in the church. My hope is that leaders will be encouraged to lead the way for the release of this encouraging gift in the Church, and in doing so will experience the untapped potential of the gift and those who function in it.

Chapter Twelve

THE PASTOR'S ROLE

ONE THING I KNOW TO BE TRUE, BOTH FROM THE SENIOR PASTOR perspective and the staff pastor perspective, is that if the senior pastor doesn't heartily bless a ministry in the church, it will not flourish. It's not enough for the pastor to *sort of* give permission to someone to start a prophecy team. For prophetic ministry to have its best results in a church, it needs the pastor's leadership and blessing. I'm not saying the pastor has to lead it or even be on a team. If he believes in it, he needs to endorse and support those who are leading it.

As a leader, the pastor will want to keep a pulse on how the ministry is progressing and to stay appraised of testimonies and possible problems. In this context, the pastor or leader must be confident enough in their calling to not be intimidated by highly prophetic people. As God-appointed leaders they have a responsibility to protect and lead their flocks in a wise way. To say that prophetic people with very strong personalities exist would be a great understatement. They may be hearing accurately and consistently, but their message may be drowned out by their insistence that their words take precedence over other's views or that they get the microphone on a regular basis.

A pastor has to be confident in his leadership so as not to be intimidated by the prophetic ones in the midst of the church. He also has to develop good relationships with the prophetic ones in his midst so the best of everyone's gifts can come forth. There are several scriptural examples of this. Zechariah and Haggai worked with Zerubbabel, the governor of Jerusalem. In the Antioch church of Acts 13, prophets and teachers worked together to build the church. We read:

> Now in the church that was at Antioch there were certain prophets and teachers: Barnabas, Simeon who was called Niger, Lucius of Cyrene, Manaen who had been brought up with Herod the tetrarch, and Saul (Acts 13:1).

Paul expounded on that model in Ephesians 4, where he identified and called the five-fold ministry to work together to equip the Church and bring it to unity and maturity in the image of Christ.

> And He Himself gave some to be apostles, some prophets, some evangelists, and some pastors and teachers, for the equipping of the saints for the work of ministry, for the edifying of the body of Christ, till we all come to the unity of the faith and of the knowledge of the Son of God, to a perfect man, to the measure of the stature of the fullness of Christ (Ephesians 4:11-13).

Most five-fold leaders will share more than one of the five-fold ministry characteristics. Some will share a pastor/prophetic anointing, while others may have an apostolic/evangelist anointing. I say this to say that many pastors may be more prophetic than they think they are, though this is not a requirement for them to lead diligently when there are prophetic people in their congregations. They will have to lead with strength and wisdom and with a good team, some possibly of high prophetic caliber.

Whatever ministry mix a leader majors in, he or she must be confident and secure in that calling. That security will help them and their team be strong in holding the line on the vision God has given without being intimidated by those who excel in ministry callings that are beyond or different from theirs.

Where leaders are secure, they lead in peace and confidence, even in the midst of warfare. They can be questioned without feeling threatened. They can be open to other viewpoints because their hearts are invested in seeing God build the best of His Kingdom by bringing out the best in each of His people.

By the same token, pastors can listen to and pray about prophetic words and input without feeling they will invoke the wrath of God by weighing them, accepting parts of some of them, and rejecting or not moving on other parts that don't fit at the moment. Where leaders are not secure, jealousy, selfish ambition, and a controlling spirit can emerge. A people-pleasing spirit may also emerge that compromises God-given vision and values to avoid confrontation and keep everyone happy.

Pastors have to be growing in their security in God as they are pastoring prophetic people. They have to learn to deal with prophetic people with encouragement and the right amount of tenderness and firmness. I say this as one whose gift mix is primarily prophetic/pastoral in its expression. I have been on both ends of giving and receiving correction in positive and negative ways. Though I learned something from every encounter, the ones that had the greatest impact are the ones that left me with hope.

Meekness, love, and humility on the part of all have to rule at the end of the day. Mike Bickle has had extensive experience as a pastor leading and developing prophetic people. He puts it this way:

God-ordained pastors are equipped to bring leaders to the church where God has placed them. They
are in a strategic position to help the church succeed
in becoming more prophetic if they wisely use their
gift of leadership. God's desire is that pastors and
prophetic people work together as a diversified team
ministry. However, more often we see insecure pastors trying to lead rejected and pushy "prophets" in a
team ministry that lacks diversity of gifting. There are
real challenges in this, but they can be overcome with
patience, humility, and careful attention to what the
Scripture teaches about how prophetic people are to be
led in relation to the larger church family.[3]

Getting Plugged In

1. Why is it important for a pastor to be secure in who
    he is and in his vision in leading and building pro-
    phetic people?

2. Name three things you feel could help pastors and
    prophetic people work together more effectively.

3. In the Mike Bickle quote, he speaks of "insecure
    pastors and pushy prophetic people." Have you ever
    witnessed this scenario? What can you do to be an
    encouragement during this type of growing process
    in the church?

Note

1. Mike Bickle, *Growing in the Prophetic: A Practical Biblical Guide to
    Dreams, Visions, and Spiritual Gifts* (Lake Mary, Florida: Charisma
    House, 2008) 126.

Chapter Thirteen

OPEN THE DOOR SLOWLY

IT SEEMS THAT WHEN NEW TRENDS HIT THE CHURCH, LEADERS often go all in. The desire for success in ministry (often described as bigger and better) can lead pastors or leaders to quickly open the door to a new concept or trend, only to find out later that no lasting fruit was produced or the desired effect wasn't achieved. I have seen the same approach with churches in opening the door to the prophetic in its many expressions. Moving in the prophetic and having a prophetic ministry are seen by some as the answer to waking up their churches or bringing in more people. This is often done without a lot of foresight into the training or the consequences resulting from a lack of vision in how prophetic ministry will integrate into the church. The results can be disastrous.

More than one church has been split by the word of the so-called *prophet*, who then goes down the street and starts his own church. We need wisdom in how to introduce and release the prophetic in the Church. I learned many of these lessons the hard way.

In one of the churches I planted, we were meeting regularly in my home. We wanted to develop a Holy Spirit/prophetic-friendly

195

culture as part of our foundation. This culture attracted others who wanted to move in this direction. A young man who appeared to be very prophetic brought his group of about ten or fifteen to join us for a few meetings. He prophesied with accuracy and seemed to have a sincere relationship with God. I was excited to see the growth in our fellowship, and we spoke of the possibility of merging our groups together.

A day or two later I received a call from his wife informing me that he was in jail. When I asked her why, she told me she had called the police because he was physically abusing her and it wasn't the first time! In my own zeal for the prophetic and to see our church grow, I almost opened the door to a situation that would have ended in disaster. I learned two valuable lessons from that experience. First, accurate prophetic words don't equal character or doctrinal substance. Second, open the door slowly on such relationships. Anyone can look good for a couple of meetings. It takes time to see what is in a person's heart and whether they truly want to build the Church or build their own ministry.

I have personally talked with many pastors and Christians whose lives were negatively affected by manipulative and inappropriate prophetic words. One Catholic priest told me he had a woman in the church who prophesied publicly her own critical feelings about the church and its leadership under the umbrella of a "thus sayeth the Lord," causing much confusion and strife. I have also known of churches who were trying to be so open to the Spirit that they became open to every person in their city who felt they were prophetic and to every practice that appeared to be prophetic in nature. This can lead to a lot of spiritual *flakiness* and the acceptance of some things that are way more the work of the flesh than the Spirit.

We need to understand that the gift of prophecy is not a trend or a buzz. It's a gift God has given to build the Church. It isn't the only gift, and a church whose only foundation is the gift of prophecy will most likely be highly unbalanced. When leaders see or experience the downsides of an unbalanced emphasis on the prophetic, they often choose to simply avoid prophetic ministry or shut it down and play it safe. Both of these responses remove the edification the prophetic can bring and the unique opportunity for involving the body in the ministry of the Spirit that the gift of prophecy can release.

THINGS TO CONSIDER

My encouragement is to open the door slowly. By this I mean that consideration and discussion should be put into integrating prophetic ministry into the church before launching prophetic ministry. Three things to consider in this process are: 1) vision and values, 2) training, and 3) ministry outlet and accountability.

The places I have seen prophetic ministry bear the most fruit are places that have already established their vision and values. God-given vision and values provide a healthy context for the prophetic to operate in. I believe that when people have a general sense of the direction a ministry is going, a natural boundary is developed for the prophetic. The individuals who come to join the staff of IHOP-KC, for example, know they are giving themselves primarily to IHOP-KC's part in the global prayer movement. Knowing this is the foundation of the ministry gives context to the prophetic ministry. People aren't going to come in and change the nature of the ministry by prophesying God is going to close the prayer room and do something else. They are going pray and listen in the context of the vision God has given the leadership. This thought is consistent with the way the OT prophets operated.

Jeremiah prophesied to Jerusalem in accordance with the covenant (vision and values) God had established with Israel. He called the Jews to return to that covenant. For post-exilic Judea, the God-given task was to rebuild Jerusalem and the temple. The prophets Haggai and Zechariah worked with Zerubbabel, the governor of

Jerusalem, and they prophesied within that context (vision and value), calling, admonishing, and encouraging the people to complete that task.

In Acts 13, prophets and teachers worked together to build the church in Antioch. This isn't to say that at times the prophetic won't challenge or give different perspective to vision and values, which can be a plus in a mature and healthy framework. Often, in these cases, it will be more about expression than philosophy. Because vision and values are generally set by church leaders to establish the course of a church, they provide a foundation of security upon which the prophetic can be built and grown in a healthy way. The lack of these things may give place for the prophetic to operate in somewhat of a void, like a carpenter trying to frame a house without a blueprint. There has to be a wineskin for the wine to flow through, and a good wineskin can stretch so as to take the best advantage of and provide the least waste of the wine. Leaders are responsible to establish the vision and values that the Holy Spirit is establishing in their work. That becomes the wineskin through which the gifts and offices of the Spirit flow to bring the church into unity, maturity, and the image of Christ.

Training is the second important factor in growing prophetic ministry in a church. Training should be clear and intentional. It should be clear in providing ministry boundaries, the mechanics of how to prophesy, and the importance of spiritual disciplines and character. Don't just think of including those who seem the most prophetic, but think of those who truly have a touch of God on their lives in the secret place. A few of the strongest prophetic people I have had on my teams in the past were people who told me they didn't think they were prophetic. One was an artist, and I could see the prophetic touch in her art. I finally talked her into joining my team, though she had her doubts. The first time she prophesied she was hooked!

The key to hearing God's voice is intimacy, and that is cultivated in the personal secret place. We ask our IHOP prophecy team members to spend four hours in prayer for every one hour they prophesy. Training should also be intentional in that it's given at specific times and the line is held that those wanting to engage in prophetic ministry go through the training.

My encouragement to those beginning this ministry in a church is to start small, with those whom the leadership has approved. Let it grow up a little in maturity before allowing it to grow up in numbers. The reason for this is that, if you open up advertising to anyone and everyone, you may end up with those in the mix who really aren't gifted but want to have influence, or those who think they are the most prophetic people in the world and you need to listen to them and heed their word (and you can be sure that you will encounter these folks somewhere along the line).

The last piece of the puzzle is to provide ministry outlet with accountability. A lady in one of my seminars once made a statement, followed by a question. She said, "I have attended many seminars and read many books on the prophetic. How do I grow in the gift?"

My answer was simple—"Prophesy." We can read all the books and go to all the conferences, but if we never open our mouth to prophesy, we will never grow in gifting. There has to be an outlet for those we train to put into practice what they have learned.

CREATING AN OUTLET FOR THE PROPHETIC

Initial training outlets can be provided through supervised ministry following scheduled training times. Those approved can also continue to grow through prophetic ministry during church altar times. Additionally, prophetic ministry should be encouraged in the marketplace, and even through planned evangelistic outreaches. However, the most consistent training will come through the development of prophesy teams. Teams can take prescheduled appointments and minister in two-hour slots.

Generally, teams are broken into groups of two to three, and they minister to groups of three about every twenty minutes for the two-hour slot. Each team should have a leader who walks their teams through briefings before and after ministering. In these briefings, they reinforce values, cover protocols, answer questions, and give counsel on how to handle different situations.

If prophetic ministry is going to grow, there has to be an outlet for people to prophesy. In developing teams, I suggest you start small, with those who are gifted, giving one person charge of the team. You may want to allow more than twenty minutes per receiving group on the front end so the teams can relax and not feel pressured to finish too quickly. Sessions can be shortened as teams gain more confidence and more people are requesting ministry.

The leader should begin each session with a briefing as described above. Accountability can be built into the process by creating "Feedback Forms" to distribute to each person receiving ministry, requesting that, following ministry time, they fill out the form and leave it at a specified location. When ministry time is finished, the team leaders review the feedback sheets with their teams. They will share the positive comments and address any negative comments with the group, using them as teaching and accountability tools. In this way, teams can be encouraged, and areas in need of growth or correction can be addressed in a team setting. It's also a helpful tool to identify those who are maturing in their gifting as well as those who may need help and direction. As values and vision, training, and outlet and accountability are put in place, the foundation for growing the prophetic in your midst will be maximized.

DEVELOPING A PROPHETIC CULTURE

Developing prophecy teams is a good way to begin prophetic ministry in the church, but prophesy teams are only one aspect of encouraging a prophetic spirit in the Church. The Holy Spirit wants to speak in so many ways and venues in both the larger corporate gathering as well as small groups, leadership meetings, and home groups.

A good way to begin is make clear to specified groups the desire to allow the Holy Spirit to move in your meetings. I say *specified* from the perspective of deciding how public you want to be initially in the beginning. You may want to begin with your leaders, or you may want to share it with the entire congregation, depending on how fast or slow you want to begin. The announcement doesn't have to be detailed. The bottom line is to simply invite and encourage the congregation to be open and hungry to see the Holy Spirit move in your midst through spiritual gifts.

Foundational to the above is to create a culture of prayer and listening. The heart of the prophetic is in being able to hear the heart of the Father. That will only happen through intentional pursuit and the investment of time on both the individual and corporate levels. One of the big hurdles to turning the corner on this is to emphasize in teaching and example the value of communion with God devotionally and in intercession. Prayer is more the last resort in the church than it is the first resort, and engaging in works is generally more highly valued than sitting before the Lord. Yet, Jesus said that His sheep know His voice. The practice of asking, listening, and praying is the foundation for hearing God's voice and receiving prophetic revelation. Preaching and teaching on fellowshipping with Christ through the Holy Spirit and making a place in service for corporate "listening" are good ways to begin to establish a corporate prophetic culture. In this framework, people can be encouraged in corporate meetings of any type to ask Jesus questions about His desires and what He might be saying for individuals and the church.

GETTING PLUGGED IN

1. Why is pastoral encouragement of the prophetic vital to the success of a growing prophetic ministry in the church?

2. How does having an established *vision/values* expression in place help nurture and define the role of the prophetic in a church?

3. What will happen to the prophetic ones in a church if there is training but not outlet for expression?

4. Why is it important that pastors be secure in who they are in God as a foundation for leading leaders?

Chapter Fourteen

MAKING ROOM FOR PROPHETIC EXPRESSION

PROPHECY TEAMS ARE ONLY ONE WAY TO BEGIN TO RELEASE THE prophetic. Another obvious place would be to encourage the release of prophetic words during church services, home groups, and youth and children's meetings. An easy way to administrate this in larger church services is to have two to three people who are available to receive prophetic words from the congregation. This team can weigh and evaluate words according to scriptural consistency, timeliness, relevance, momentary weight and confirmation, and general agreement (a number of words on the same theme).

Then, these words can be related to the leader on the platform and can then be administrated in a number of ways. For example, the one who had the word may give it, several integrated words may be related together in a summary, the leader may release the appropriate words himself, etc. On occasion where the words all confirm the message the pastor is going to preach, the words may serve to encourage and confirm what the pastor already has on his heart.

The last thing to consider is the congregational response to the prophetic words. What is God saying through those words? Is He simply encouraging the congregation? Is He asking for a response? This is for the pastoral team to decide, and then the pastor can call on the congregation for the appropriate response, which in some cases could result in an altar call, while in other cases may simply call for an "Amen, we receive this, Lord" type of response.

Some might argue against this type of administration in larger meetings from the perspective that it might limit the gift, short-circuit the spontaneity of the Holy Spirit, or quench the fire of the messenger. My experience actually proves the opposite. Paul said that "the spirits of the prophets are subject to the prophets" (1 Cor. 14:32), meaning that the one who has the message also has the ability to release it in a timely and orderly way. Paul also suggests that two to three prophets speak, possibly indicating that like tongues and interpretation, prophetic messages be limited to three. He said, "Let two or three prophets speak, and let the others judge" (1 Cor. 14:29).

In a service where the Holy Spirit is moving and ten to fifteen people may have prophetic words, you must have a means of discerning the heart of those messages and then delivering that which will most be in line with what the Holy Spirit is saying to edify the church in the most impactful way. In this way, the church receives the fullness of the prophetic word, and prophetic people learn to seek the edification of the church as their primary goal in giving words.

In First Thessalonians 5:19-21, Paul commanded the church not to put out the Spirit's fire or despise prophecy. Prophecy done rightly increases the Spirit's fire in our midst. Prophecy done wrongly diminishes the fire and causes people to despise it.

I believe there are three things that contribute to people despising prophecy. One is prophetic words that are overly demanding and manipulative. Another is prophetic words that give a time frame for fulfillment that do not come to pass, and the last is words that are weak, containing a lot of fluff and flattery but not much substance. If a congregation gets a steady diet of these types of words, they will eventually stop listening, resulting in a despising of the prophetic. For this reason, administering words in some fashion as described above is helpful for gleaning the best of the prophetic that will increase the Spirit's fire and lead to the highest edification of the Church.

Administration in home groups can be less structured as they are usually smaller and function on a different level of community. This can be a good place for people to begin to experiment with the prophetic. They can be encouraged, and gently corrected if need be, and can have a safe place to grow in their gift.

Administration in youth and children's meetings can also be done differently, depending on size and goals. I encourage the release of the prophetic on the next generation as they will be leading the Church in the blink of an eye. There is no Junior Holy Spirit. The same Spirit that inhabits and speaks through adult believers also lives and speaks through young believers.

My youngest son was eight years old when he joined my prophecy team and prophesied with accuracy over those who came through our teams. It's often easier to train these young ones to hear, and once they do they can have many years to cultivate the gift and their character. After a simple way of administering the prophetic in these services is established, the children and youth can learn to prophesy and build the church through their gift.

Music is another area where the gift of prophecy can be developed and released. One of the earliest mentions of the corporate release of the prophetic goes back to the establishment of the Tabernacle of David, where prophetic singers and musicians were set apart to minister to the Lord in David's house of prayer. God created music to move our hearts to Him, and then His own heart is moved by our music! It's the antiphonal song from His heart to our hearts, then back to His heart. For this reason, the prophetic and music go together like the waves and the shore.

Several years ago I had a dream in which I was in a large, round college classroom. I was in a guitar class full of both believers and unbelievers. Class was about to begin, and everyone was tuning their electric guitars and practicing little riffs and leads. The professor walked in and went to the front and got everyone's attention. There was a large-screen TV in the front of the room, and he put in a VCR tape and told the class, "I want you to see this guitar player. He is the absolute best." He turned on the TV and the tape began. The picture was focused on the guitarist's finger work. He was so fast and clean it was almost hard to see his fingers move. The music was unlike any music anyone had ever heard before. Beyond original, beyond what anyone could even conceive of. The whole class, believers and unbelievers alike, stood transfixed, mouths hanging open. All were saying how amazing this guy was, and wondered who he was. The picture began to pan to a larger view, and you could see the guitarist's face. In the dream, when I saw His face, I cried out, "It's Jesus!" It was the Lord, ripping it up on the guitar. The whole class knew it was Him and just stood there in amazement.

God wants to release to the Church the sounds of heaven, both lyrically and musically. In Revelation the saints sing a new song. Why spend time trying to copy the world's music when God, who is the author of music, wants to release the new sounds and the new songs that will reveal Him and touch a generation? He wants to break into our worship with prophetic songs and prophetic oracles that are sung to release His presence and power and healing and deliverance.

When David spoke in the Psalms of *songs of deliverance,* he wasn't coining a nice phrase. He was talking about prophetic singers and musicians who could shift the heavens both spiritually and naturally (see Ps. 40:1-3; 69:30-33; 144:1-2). Music moves His heart and brings the release of the Kingdom. David's music had the power to drive Saul's demons away. I believe there is a sound yet coming that, when sung in the midst of God's people, it will give a tangible, musical expression to Isaiah 61. The anointing will be released and prisoners will be released and captives will go free. Beauty will be released for ashes, joy for weeping, laughing for sorrow, and thanksgiving for the spirit of heaviness.

As singers and musicians seek God's face, He will release to them the prophetic sounds of heaven. Leaders need to be willing to allow this prophetic expression in music to come forth. The relationship between pastor, worship leader and prophetic singers, and musicians is key in developing this aspect of the prophetic. Working together to administrate this side of the prophetic can bring great encouragement and fire to the Church.

PROPHETIC COUNCILS

When there are enough mature prophetic individuals, a prophetic council could be formed. This is a loosely-knit group that would be invited to pray prophetically into the direction and needs of the Church, the city, and the region.

Such a group would ask questions like: What are the prophetic promises over the area? What are the watchmen seeing? Is the Lord calling for the release of any prophetic acts (forgiveness, reconciliation, cleansing, etc.)?

People with other gift mixes could also be part of this group. The goal would be to have a Holy Ghost *think tank* to see and hear what the Lord is saying, and then to get direction on how to administrate it.

REGIONAL PROPHETIC INTERCESSION

Regional or city intercession can also be embraced in the prophetic. With this type of intercession, it's important to understand what the prophetic promises over your region or city are. Insight into what the enemy's plans are in the region can also be helpful, though the major emphasis is in lifting Jesus high and declaring His promises in the city.

Besides doing research in the natural, the Holy Spirit may reveal His plans and heart. He may indicate the calling of key prophetic prayer meetings that bring churches into the unity of intercession. This may be expressed in prayer walks or symbolic prophetic acts that He may reveal and encourage.

I believe God will raise up the Isaiah 28:5 and Psalm 24:7 prophetic intercessors to turn back the battle at the gate and bring in the King of glory through worship and prayer. We read this in the following:

> In that day the Lord of hosts will be for a crown of glory and a diadem of beauty to the remnant of His people, for a spirit of justice to him who sits in judgment, and for strength to those who turn back the battle at the gate (Isaiah 28:5-6).

> Lift up your heads, O you gates! And be lifted up, you everlasting doors! And the King of glory shall come in. Who is this King of glory? The Lord strong and mighty, the Lord mighty in battle. Lift up your heads, O you gates! Lift up, you everlasting doors! And the King of glory shall come in. Who is this King of glory? The Lord of hosts, He is the King of glory (Psalm 24:7-10).

OTHER PROPHETIC EXPRESSIONS

Speaking prophetic words to individuals or groups in the church is just one aspect of prophesying. There are other expressions as well.

The Arts

God also wants to release the prophetic in the area of the arts (drama, dance, art). Because prophetic revelation comes to us as the thoughts of God, He can download entire prophetic concepts for the arts that can be expressed through the mediums listed above.

Why should Hollywood have a monopoly on creativity? The Church is barely scratching the surface of impact in these areas. God wants to redeem the arts along with a generation whose hearts are connected so much to the visual aspect of life.

Dance is another area. I believe He not only wants to redeem a hip hop culture, He wants to give original music and dance that will release joy and set people free. We need to give God space to move in dance as He wants. It seems funny to me the ways in which some of the Church views dance. If it's flowery and ballet-like, it's holy. But if it's crumping or hip hop or break dancing it must be of the devil!

Obviously, there are certain types of dance movements in all arenas that are sensual and have no place in prophetic expression. But God wants to reach all generations through prophetic dance, and we need to be open to see what He is doing prophetically and encourage and bless it.

Social Media

Prophetic communications is another way the gift can be released. There are many social networking opportunities available. There are those looking for a pulpit to deliver their prophetic messages, and they can find a ready-made pulpit and audience through web sites, Facebook, YouTube, Twitter, and personal blogging sites. The possibilities are endless. Church bulletins and publications can also be used as a means of expression for written prophetic messages.

Prophetic Evangelism

Evangelism is a great place to encourage and release the prophetic. IHOP-KC has had teams go to the Kansas City Psychic Fair to do dream interpretation. They set up their own table as the *Mystics of Yeshua* and had great success interpreting dreams and prophesying over those who stopped by, leading some to the Lord. They were listed by many as their favorites at the fair, one reason being that they didn't charge money for their prophetic words.

The IHOP evangelism teams regularly do outreaches, and prophesying over unbelievers is a common part of the outreach. However, prophetic evangelism doesn't have to be an organized event. As people are growing in their gifts, there is no reason they can't get a word for someone at Wal-Mart or at their place of business or at school or for their neighbors. I have prophesied to unbelievers on planes, trains, street corners, golf courses, at McDonald's, hospitals, and many other places. While the people I prophesy to don't always get saved, they are almost always moved by the fact that God knows them, loves them, and cares about them. It moves their hearts that much closer and prepares them to be more receptive to the gospel.

As leaders, we need to be open to the many ways God wants to release the prophetic in our churches. When we recognize those with gifts, we need to provide a variety of outlets to direct them to and coach them in. Often, they will come to us. All these possibilities can help us open the door that just may be key to helping them fulfill their destinies in God in regard to their prophetic gifts and calling.

GETTING PLUGGED IN

1. Make a list of the different arenas that are available to you personally to prophesy in, and make a list of the different avenues of prophetic expression you feel are part of your life/ministry. Then, make a plan, including timetables, to implement the other two lists into your daily life.

2. What can you do to help develop a prophetic culture in your area of influence?

Chapter Fifteen

GROWING PROPHETIC PEOPLE

As you have been reading this book, you may have been considering how you would start prophetic ministry in your area of leadership. Most likely, you know people who are prophetic even if they are in an undeveloped stage. There will be those who will try to convince you that they are prophetic (and may very well be), and there will be those you will convince they are prophetic because they don't think they are. This will be an ongoing process.

As the process begins and conversation gets underway, there are two things to keep in mind. One is the target. What are we aiming our prophetic groups at? Second, we want to have some training exercises that help people grow, learn to listen, and practice their prophetic gifts. The first part of this chapter will help establish the target, and the second part will focus on practical training.

PROPHETS AND THE GIFT OF PROPHECY

Two scriptures that help establish the target are First Corinthians 14:3 and Ephesians 4:11-16. I have already touched on both of these, but to summarize, First Corinthians 14:3 gives personal guidelines to the prophesier. The ground rules are simple—edify, encourage, and strengthen. The verses in Ephesians go toward a bigger, broader view of the corporate purpose of having active, functioning prophetic people in your church. Paul is defining the purposes of the five-fold ministry in these verses, and prophets are part of that description. Shortly, I will discuss the subject of prophets, but the goal for prophetic people, even though most of them are not prophets, is to use their gifts to accomplish, in some measure, that which prophets are called to do in these verses.

Many authors have addressed the subject of prophets today on a grand scale, so I won't devote a lot of time to the subject here. My thoughts are ordered more toward the practical job description of prophets and how that affects the church in general and those who are growing in their prophetic gifts specifically.

First, I believe there are and will continue to be prophets simply because Scripture has given no indication that there is an end to this office or ministry. We know of Agabus in Acts 11. Paul spoke of teachers and prophets in the Antioch Church in Acts 13. There were prophets in the church of Corinth (see 1 Cor. 14), and Paul lists prophets along with apostles, pastors, teachers, and evangelists in his description of the five-fold ministry (see Eph. 4). They are included in the Word, and for that reason I believe prophets are still part of the makeup of the Church. I have known a few people whom I would classify as prophets because they fulfilled the job description given by Paul for prophets in Ephesians 4. I think as the Church matures and the times require, we will see an increase of godly, accurate, servant-hearted prophets given as gifts to the Church.

Second, with this idea in mind, there needs to be some definition of what a NT prophet is, so that in expectation and training we have a definite goal to shoot for, even if it is general in nature. One of the first things to recognize is the difference between NT and OT prophets. Confusion on this subject can lead to misunderstanding, division, and brokenness in both the church and the prophet.

Similarities between OT and NT Prophets

- Prophets are called by God, not by human choice. Many of the prophets relate an experience with God that set them apart (see Isa. 6; Jer. 1; Ezek. 1, 2; John the Baptist, Luke 1). It isn't just about gifting, it's also about calling.

- Prophets demonstrated holy character. This isn't to say they were perfect and didn't struggle with human weakness, but they were wholehearted in their pursuit of righteousness and strove to please the Lord in their lifestyles.

- Prophets were servants of God. Nineteen times OT Scripture makes reference to "My servants the prophets." In the NT, the prophet was to be a servant of the Bride and friend of the Bridegroom—building, encouraging, and strengthening the church. Old and NT prophets were servants and messengers of God.

- Prophets accurately foretold coming events. Old and NT Prophets had aspects of "foretelling" in their messages. For example, Jeremiah's prophecy of seventy years of captivity (see Jer. 25:11) and Agabus's prophecy of a coming famine (Acts 11:28).

Differences between OT and NT Prophets

- OT prophets were few in number and were called primarily to prophesy to Israel, Judah, and often many other nations. While their messages were directed to all, they were very often focused on leaders (kings,

priests, prophets, princes, governors). NT prophets
primarily prophesied to the church and gave themselves to equipping the saints. (One exception would
be John in Revelation 10:11, being commanded to
prophesy to nations in the context of the end-time
message and Christ's return.) With the fulfillment
of Joel's prophecy, the Holy Spirit was available to
all believers, resulting in a general increase of a prophetic spirit on the whole Church and an increase in
the number of prophets as well.

- OT prophets had direct divine revelation (see 2 Pet.
  1:21) and so carried divine authority on their words.
  Their prophecies were considered the very words of
  God and weren't to be debated, weighed, or argued
  with. To disobey the word of the prophet was to
  disobey God. The words of NT prophets were not
  considered to carry the same authority. That is why
  they were to be weighed and judged by the congregation (see 1 Cor. 14:29; 1 Thess. 5:19-21). The words of
  NT prophets were not recorded or considered to be
  on the same level as Scripture. I like the way Mike
  Bickle states it in his book *Growing in the Prophetic.*

  In the OT there was "prophetic concentration,"
  and in the NT there was "prophetic distribution."
  The fate of the church would never depend on the
  accuracy of one prophet. With potentially several
  or even a number of prophets in each geographic
  location, the same kind of accuracy of revelation
  is not needed because of the safeguard of other
  prophets' mandate to judge each other's words
  and even Spirit anointed believers' ability to test,
  discern, confirm or deny a claim of revelation.[1]

- The validity of an OT prophet was determined by the exact fulfillment of his prophetic words (those given about specific events in specific time frames). Jeremiah prophesied that the false prophet Hananiah would die within the year. If Hananiah had not died, Jeremiah would have been declared a false prophet, worthy of being put to death (see Jer. 28:15-17). This is confirmed by Moses in Deuteronomy:

  But the prophet who presumes to speak a word in My name, which I have not commanded him to speak, or who speaks in the name of other gods, that prophet shall die. ...When a prophet speaks in the name of the Lord, if the thing does not happen or come to pass, that is the thing which the Lord has not spoken; the prophet has spoken it presumptuously; you shall not be afraid of him (Deuteronomy 18:20,22).

- NT prophets' prophecies (the book of Acts and beyond) did not have to be perfectly accurate, and again, the church was encouraged to weigh their words (see 1 Cor. 14:29; 1 Thess. 5:20-21). While the word of Agabus was fulfilled in Paul's life in a general way, it did not happen exactly the way he prophesied it (see Acts 21:10-14, 27-33). However this did not appear to have any bearing on his status as a prophet.

IN SUMMARY

So we see there are major differences in the roles and the authority of OT and NT prophets. It doesn't mean NT prophets can't do the miracles OT prophets did or receive accurate prophetic information like they did. It just means NT prophets won't carry the same "Thus saith the Lord" authority that the

OT prophets carried or have the same authority in terms of their words being equal with Scripture.

No single prophet's words today are above being weighed and judged. Instead, they, along with the rest of the five-fold ministry, are support roles for the foundation that has already been laid in Christ. My purpose in addressing this isn't merely academic. The importance of the subject goes to establishing boundaries and definitions for prophetic people who may join themselves to our churches. Those who view their prophetic calling through an OT lens are more likely to carry the conceptions that they have *the* Word of the Lord, and there is no debating it. "Thus saith the Lord," take it or leave it. They may be less tolerant toward those they deem to be less gifted, and sometimes the desire for recognition and position are part of the package. Leaders must have a comprehensive view and conviction on this subject to gently teach, lead, and guide the prophetic ones in their midst.

THE PROPHET'S JOB DESCRIPTION

The job description for prophets is found in Ephesians 4. This is the target we are aiming at with training.

> So Christ himself gave the apostles, the prophets, the evangelists, the pastors and teachers, to equip his people for works of service, so that the body of Christ may be built up until we all reach unity in the faith and in the knowledge of the Son of God and become mature, attaining to the whole measure of the fullness of Christ. Then we will no longer be infants, tossed back and forth by the waves, and blown here and there by every wind of teaching and by the cunning and craftiness of people in their deceitful scheming. Instead, speaking the truth in love, we will grow to become in every respect the mature body of him who is the head, that is, Christ. From him the whole body, joined and held together by every supporting

ligament, grows and builds itself up in love, as each part does its work (Ephesians 4:11-16 NIV).

Here Paul paints a picture of the church as the body of Christ. As each member does its work, the end result will be a mature, spotless Bride that functions powerfully under Christ's headship, moving in unity and love, preparing the way and crying out for Christ's return. Foundational to this picture is the role of the five-fold ministry in equipping the Bride to reach the goal. Because our focus is on prophets and the prophetic, I will limit my comments to that sphere.

The role of the NT prophet is:

- To equip the church for works of ministry. This means that the prophet doesn't just prophesy, he trains others to prophesy. He equips and trains the church to hear the voice of God and walk in discernment. This would infer, at least to some degree, some instructional ability on the part of the prophet, as training and equipping require the ability to instruct. This doesn't have to be line upon line with perfect teaching notes and would probably look different with different personalities, but the ability to model and instruct would go along with the equipping.

- To edify the body of Christ. This means that the prophet would prophesy, both individually and corporately, timely and encouraging words that would edify the whole church. At times this could include signs and wonders and the accurate foretelling of future events. In some situations he/she may privately admonish (strongly warn or rebuke) those who continued in a sin, in a redemptive way with a redemptive heart. This could also include giving a prophetic "heads up" in meetings with leaders, for possible season changes or new things that are on the horizon for the church. Some prophetic ministers might function beyond the body of Christ to touch the arena of secular government or business upon invitation, giving prophetic counsel to those in authority and leadership.

- To pursue and promote unity, faith, and maturity by serving the church in ministry and by personal example. Jesus's testimony is the Spirit of prophecy and prophetic gifting and character merge in His example. Prophets are gifts to the Bride to serve as examples in service and love, demonstrating faith and maturity. They are given to bring the Church together, not separate it. When they do their job right, the Church will love Jesus more. To quote Bickle again:

  In other words, prophecy is not to be seen as an end in itself or as that which simply makes church meetings more exciting. It is the gas that fuels the tank of intercession, purity, and more effective outreach to others.[2]

- To demonstrate a grounded, biblical approach to life. They are to be students of the Word of God and should be devoted to prayer. Their words and their lives should encourage the childish to grow up, the weak to persevere, the unstable to find deep-rooted faith so as to avoid being deceived, and the rank and file to keep the fire burning in the midst of the mundane.

The key characteristic of the office will be deep friendship with God. Several years ago the Lord spoke to me about prophetic friendship, using the apostle John as an example, and I knew there were three aspects of prophetic growth related to John as Jesus's friend. The first aspect was tied to the gospel of John and was connected to renewing and restoring the love and wonder of the cross, resulting in deeper obedience and gratitude to Jesus (see John 15).

The second aspect involved four areas of preparation in connection with John's letters. The first was the call to deeper holiness among a prophetic people (see 1 John 2:4-6). The second was the call to a prophetic people to walk in community in the light with one another (see 1 John 2:8-10). The third was growth in increased discernment about our times (see 1 John 4:1-6). The fourth was connected to a greater release of power through prophetic people in the church (see 1 John 3:8). The last aspect was tied to John's revelation of the testimony of Jesus in Revelation 19:10. Prophetic friends will prepare the Bride to receive the Bridegroom by strengthening and alerting the Bride to be diligent and watchful as the return of the Lord draws closer. All these aspects of revelation come to us through John, the disciple whom Jesus loved. As Jesus's friends, the prophets are to build a "house of friends and a family of affection" whose hearts will be alive and burning with fiery love unto the Lord's return.

Will there be prophets in every church? Most likely not, but every church can have those who are highly gifted prophetically and who, with the right training, can still serve in a highly prophetic capacity. This is why the equipping perspective is so important.

ALLOWING ROOM FOR GROWTH: THE DISTINCTION BETWEEN IMMATURE PROPHETIC PEOPLE AND FALSE PROPHETS

The basic training for prophets and those desiring to grow in the gift of prophecy are the same. In most cases, you won't know if someone you are training is a prophet or is simply highly gifted prophetically until their gift emerges in the midst of training and community life. Even if a person has a revelation that they are called to the office, it may take years for the fullness of the gift and the character to come to the place where consistent, fruitful revelation come forth to build the body.

So we aim everyone at the Ephesians 4 job description and help them mature in loving, equipping, and grounding the saints in the Word of the Lord through the gift of prophecy. As we move in this direction, everyone will make mistakes as they step out and take risks. They may miss it between what they hear and how they interpret and prophesy. They may miss it in the area of their timing, either in a word being fulfilled or in the timing of giving a word. They may get overzealous in the insistence of a word being received and action taken immediately.

There are lots of ways mistakes can be made. When someone misses it, does this mean they are a false prophet? Probably not. It simply means they are trying to grow in their gift and calling. If we give them room to grow and throw in some encouragement and solid, diligent training, maturity will be within their grasp.

HOW DO WE KNOW FALSE PROPHETS?

There are two biblical criteria for recognizing false prophets, and they are consistent in both the OT and the NT. The first is discerning the source of their prophecies and the second is looking at their lifestyles (fruit). Consider the following scriptures:

> The word of the Lord came to me: "Son of man, prophesy against the prophets of Israel who are now prophesying. Say to those who prophesy out of their own imagination: 'Hear the word of the Lord! This is what the Sovereign Lord says: Woe to the foolish prophets who follow their own spirit and have seen nothing! Your prophets, Israel, are like jackals among ruins. You have not gone up to the breaches in the wall to repair it for the people

of Israel so that it will stand firm in the battle on the day of the Lord. Their visions are false and their divinations a lie. Even though the Lord has not sent them, they say, "The Lord declares," and expect him to fulfill their words" (Ezekiel 13:1-6 NIV).

Ezekiel identified three characteristics of false prophets in these verses. They spoke out of their own spirit (desires and agendas), not from the heart of the Lord. They had no spirit of prayer to stand in the gap with compassion and encouragement for the people of God. They spoke from a spirit of divination (an antichrist spirit) designed to lead the people away from God and His purposes.

Jeremiah touched on the same themes and added another distinction of false prophets.

"For both prophet and priest are profane; yes, in My house I have found their wickedness," says the Lord. "...They prophesied by Baal and caused My people Israel to err...They commit adultery and walk in lies; they also strengthen the hands of evildoers, so that no one turns back from his wickedness...." Thus says the Lord of hosts: "Do not listen to the words of the prophets who prophesy to you...I have not sent these prophets, yet they ran. I have not spoken to them, yet they prophesied. But if they had stood in My counsel, and had caused My people to hear My words, then they would have turned them from their evil way...." Indeed they are prophets of the deceit of their own heart, who try to make My people forget My name by their dreams which everyone tells his neighbor, as their fathers forgot My name for Baal" (Jeremiah 23:11,13-14,16,21-22,26-27).

Jeremiah pointed out that not only did false prophets speak out of their own imaginations and an antichrist spirit, but their lifestyles were wicked. They committed adultery, perverted justice, and strengthened those who ran into sin. So the two criteria—prophesying from a false source and bearing bad fruit—are both listed by Jeremiah in his description of the prophets of the day.

These same concepts are carried into the NT. Both Jude and Peter addressed this subject as demonstrated in the scriptures below.

> *In the very same way, on the strength of their dreams these ungodly people pollute their own bodies, reject authority and heap abuse on celestial beings. ...These people slander whatever they do not understand, and the very things they do understand by instinct—as irrational animals do—will destroy them. Woe to them! They have taken the way of Cain; they have rushed for profit into Balaam's error; they have been destroyed in Korah's rebellion. These people are blemishes at your love feasts...shepherds who feed only themselves* (Jude 8, 10-12 NIV).

> *But there were also false prophets among the people, even as there will be false teachers among you, who will secretly bring in destructive heresies.... By covetousness they will exploit you with deceptive words....They are spots and blemishes, carousing in their own deceptions while they feast with you, having eyes full of adultery and that cannot cease from sin, enticing unstable souls.... They have forsaken the right way and gone astray, following the way of Balaam the son of Beor, who loved the wages of unrighteousness* (2 Peter 2:1,3,13-15).

The same two characteristics that are highlighted in the OT are brought to the surface here—the source of their teaching and "swelling words," and their selfish, sinful lifestyles. Unfortunately, these things may not be immediately apparent. Both Peter and

Jude described them as "blemishes on your love feasts," giving the indication that they lived among the believing community and were not immediately recognized and restrained.

A man or woman may show up in a church and outwardly appear to be spiritual and willing to prophesy and be the pastor's best friend and supporter. They may even prophesy something that appears to come to pass. Moses told us in Deuteronomy 13:1-15 that a false prophet may actually prophesy accurately, but not by the Spirit of God. It is all part of the deceptive spirit. Outwardly, they may look righteous while inside there are all the characteristics of the ungodly wisdom and ambition that James describes (see James 3:14-16). Yet many pastors, eager to have some help and support and wanting to be open to the prophetic, make a way for such people before they have time to test their fruit. By the time they begin to see what is happening, the damage has already begun to be unleashed.

This is why in-house training and accountability really serve to strengthen the church and the prophetic together. It gives time to observe people in training and time to watch and test the fruit in the context of how people live in community. This gives space and place to do as John said:

> Dear friends, do not believe every spirit, but test the spirits to see whether they are from God, because many false prophets have gone out into the world (1 John 4:1 NIV).

> Little children, it is the last hour; and as you have heard that the Antichrist is coming, even now many antichrists have come, by which we know that it is the last hour. ...But you have an anointing from the Holy One, and you know all things (1 John 2:18,20).

We need the Holy Spirit, the Word of God, and the gift of discerning of spirits to keep the gates closed to such people. We need the spirit of the watchman, as described in Isaiah 21:5, to see the works of the enemy and turn back the battle at the gate. We need to live in the Word and the Spirit to be able to discern not only the word, but also the spirit behind the word, as Jeremiah has said:

> "Let the prophet who has a dream recount the dream, but let the one who has my word speak it faithfully. For what has straw to do with grain?" declares the Lord. "Is not my word like fire," declares the Lord, "and like a hammer that breaks a rock in pieces?" (Jeremiah 23:28-29 NIV)

Jeremiah is saying that the one who knows and has the Word of the Lord in him will be able to discern between the wheat and the chaff in the prophetic realm.

GETTING PLUGGED IN

1. What two scriptures give the target/goal for prophetic ministry?

2. How is having a target to aim at helpful for prophetic growth?

3. In looking at the job description for prophets and prophetic people, what aspects do you see as being the most challenging?

4. What is the difference between an immature prophesier and a false prophet?

NOTES

1. Bickle, *Growing in the Prophetic*, 51.
2. Ibid., 78.

Chapter Sixteen

PRACTICAL TRAINING

THE TRAINING PROCESS IS THE SAME FOR PROPHETS AND THOSE with prophetic gifting. Most leaders think of prophets only from the perspective of the mature man of God ministering on the platform. Their ministry is powerful and edifying, and pastors would love to have them as part of their churches. This will rarely happen, and if it does, that prophet probably won't be there much because of the greater calling to the body of Christ. Most likely, a mature prophet is not going to just show up. What do we do?

We start where we are. You might have a seven-year-old prophet sitting in your pews! He doesn't know it yet and you don't know it yet, but there he sits. There is a lyric in one of Keith Green's songs, "Prophets don't grow up from little boys, do they?"[1] Yes, they do! Having foundational training in place will provide an opportunity for prophets and prophetic people to emerge. This will help provide outlets for ministry while also developing personal character. Staying steady with this will open the gate for steady growth and maturity. My friend Julie Meyer had a dream that goes to the heart of this. I relate only a part of the dream below as she told it:

> We were in a room, like a courtroom and Jesus was standing at the head of the table. He had a gavel, like one you pound on the desk of a judge when court is beginning to start. He said, "The Prophets are coming. The Prophets are coming. Just as the singers, musicians, and intercessors are coming, so are the Prophets. What do you have set in place to govern the hearts of the Prophets. If you have nothing in place, this will be the outcome."

> Then, Jesus turned on a movie for all of us to watch. [There were] hundreds of oxen. They were messy. They were loud. They were making this sound, whatever it is that oxen say, that is what they were doing, but they were all trying to be louder than each other, and they were all trying to get through this small gate at the same time. So they were all getting stuck but even though they were stuck, they still all kept trying to push their way through the small gate at the same time.

> Jesus said again, "What do you have set in place to govern the hearts of the prophets? They are coming. They are arising."[2]

What a challenging and haunting question for the Church today! How will we respond?

PRACTICAL TRAINING FOR DEVELOPING PROPHETIC PEOPLE

We have discussed the target we are aiming at; now we will look at the equipping side of the goal. My suggestion is to begin with small groups. This allows for a safe atmosphere where people can step out and gain confidence in prophesying. It also allows for accountability and feedback, both of which are vital to growing in the gift. Depending on the size of the training group, it may be good to have a couple of leaders there to help with the practical exercises.

There is a wide range of training materials available to develop the gift, including what is in this book. Three aspects that deserve ongoing development and training are revelation and interpretation, character and service, and continual practical ministry.

By revelation and interpretation, I am speaking of the different ways we hear God and how we interpret what He is saying. It is likely you will have people hearing on a multitude of levels, such as dreams and visions, phrases and impressions, pictures, etc. Walking the group through the different ways they hear and helping them make sense of it can be really helpful. This will often help to determine what you do with prophetic information (intercede, prophesy in a corporate or one-on-one setting, share with leadership, etc.). This can also help prophetic people develop their prophetic language (learning to understand the particular ways God speaks to them on a regular basis). Taking time to walk through some examples as a group is both fun and helpful. Here are a few other activities that can help develop hearing and prophesying.

Prophetic Treasure Hunts

People are the treasures; the group is listening for the clues. The simplest way to begin is to select a place to go. The group prays together and asks two questions. Who and what? The *who* is connected to a person the Holy Spirit will highlight and the team will search for (e.g., a woman in her thirties or an older gentleman). The *what* goes to that which will highlight them so the prophesiers will recognize them. The color pink, a black purse, and carrying a little boy would be descriptive phrases that highlight the person— in this case, the woman in her thirties.

When the list is compiled, the group goes to the chosen destination and begins to look for the person who was highlighted, using the prophetic clues they received in prayer. When people are found who fit the clues, the team breaks the ice and begins to minister and prophesy to them. This format can be tweaked and used in different ways. For example, instead of choosing a destination, during prayer the group could ask the Lord to highlight a place or an address or a street. The goal of the exercise is twofold. One is to teach the group to listen to the Holy Spirit and the second is to bless someone through a prophetic word.

Rotate the Prophesier

Form the training group into a circle of six to ten people, all facing inward. If you have more people, form them into two groups. Choose one person from the group and have them stand in the center with their eyes closed. Spin them a few times and stop when they are facing one particular person. While their eyes are closed, ask them a few questions about the person they are facing, such as is the person a male or a female (I correct them immediately if they are wrong, to help them stay on track and to stay gender sensitive), or what month the person was born in, or what is the person's spiritual gift, etc., and then I have them add anything else they want. When they are finished, have them open their eyes to see who they prophesied over and get some feedback.

Then, have the two people trade places and start again. Repeat until everyone has prophesied.

You can also reverse the flow of the group by having the person in the middle close his eyes and stand still while the outer circle rotates. The purpose of this exercise is to help people learn to listen and prophesy without seeing the person he is prophesying to. This teaches people not to judge by outer appearance but rather to learn to depend on the voice of the Holy Spirit. Most of the time, people miss it on one of the questions. When they do, encourage them to continue to focus on hearing God's voice and jump back in.

Rapid Fire Prophesy

Choose two to three people to stand before the group. Have the group prophesy over them in one-sentence prophecies. This helps people contextualize their word to speak it in the shortest and clearest form. This can also be done by assigning the group single questions to ask God about each of those in the front of the room (e.g., what book of the Bible does God want to speak to them about, or if Jesus was standing in front of them right now, what would He want to say to them?). When the exercise is completed, ask the people who received words to give feedback. This exercise teaches the group to ask specific questions and listen for answers to specific questions.

Prophecy Lines

Divide the group into two lines and have them face each other. As in the previous exercise, assign questions for each person to ask God about the person he or she is facing. You can use the list at the end of chapter two to draw from. After one line has prophesied, have the opposite line do the same. As time permits, you can then have one of the lines move up one person and begin again.

Question and Answer

This is an exercise that can be given as homework. Ask each person to choose a group context they are familiar with in which to prophesy (church, marketplace, classroom). They are to ask the Lord to highlight to them one person in that group they are to prophesy to. Using the list at the end of chapter one, have them ask God in their private time each of the questions in relation to the person who has been highlighted to them, encouraging them not to spend more than thirty seconds waiting for an answer (the Holy Spirit will answer the relevant ones for them at the time).

Have them record their answers on their paper. When they are finished, have them go to the person and share what they received and get feedback on how they did. This exercise will help the group with specific listening and interpreting skills.

These are just a few exercises to use to develop a listening ear. While they might seem like games, they are actually teaching people to dial down, in slightly pressured situations, and listen to God.

Character and Service

The focus here is on helping prophetic people go deep into God's heart, His Word, and His character. The key here, as has been previously addressed, is growing in intimacy with Christ. I like to encourage people to spend four hours in prayer for every one hour they prophesy. A good way to begin to develop this is to take a portion of every meeting to break out and meditate and pray through a passage of Scripture. You can use your own model or the one in this book.

Have everyone use the same verse. Give about twenty minutes for this exercise and then add another ten minutes or so for group discussion about what they are receiving. Encourage the group to practice this exercise daily.

Along with this, there are particular areas that prophetic people can get attacked in, that they can avoid if they develop the right perspective. I have listed them to contrast the negative and the positive: pride/humility, elitism/servanthood, and sensuality/spirituality. Looking at these subjects through a variety of lenses can help lay solid foundations to help your group avoid the pitfalls of many who have gone before as well as establishing tools and mindsets to overcome and develop godly character.

I would also recommend you add planned acts of service. Try some acts of kindnesses along with the prophetic ministry—raking someone's leaves, preparing meals, or visiting people in rest homes or hospitals. Other possibilities are taking on a project for the local church like home cleanup, yard work, landscaping, painting, etc. These activities underscore the truth that the gift of prophecy is, at its heart, a servant gift, working in conjunction with other gifts to build the Church. It's not just about the glory of serving in the gift of prophecy; it's about a lifestyle of serving.

Continual Practical Ministry

This is where we find a place to release people to prophesy. I previously mentioned that one of the best ways to do this is through prophecy teams. Another place to release this is in altar ministry following church services. You can also set up times to bless church departments or marketplace people through prophetic ministry. For example, having a specific ministry time when your Christian Education department can soak in God's presence and receive prophetic ministry. The possibilities are limitless.

A Simple Model for Meetings

You can break down the group time in thirds, giving a third of the time to prophetic exercise and/or discussion on interpretive skills, a third to meditating on Scripture, and a third to discussion on character issues and subjects. You can add a few minutes on the back end to discuss servanthood and practical ministry projects. You can also give place, as some are maturing in their gift, to allow them to teach a small portion, or do some personal prophetic ministry and then give feedback. Make the meetings fun, challenging, and interactive so the group stays engaged and connected.

SUMMARY

I cannot tell you how many leaders I know who have been blessed through and encouraged by prophetic ministry. When done right, the Church can grow and be inspired and strengthened in the power of the Holy Spirit through developing, maturing prophetic ministry. Individual lives are encouraged as they see the impact they can have as believers functioning in the gift of prophecy. It will take time and work to grow the prophetic ministry in your church or group, and though at times it can be a little messy, it is well worth the investment. This is the "jumping in" place, the "rubber meets the road" place. May the Lord bless you with grace, wisdom, tenderness, and an increased spirit of revelation as you begin the journey!

NOTES

1. Keith Green, "Song for My Parents," *For Him Who Has Ears to Hear* (Universal Music, Brentwood Benson Publ., Ears To Hear Music, Birdwing Music, 1977).

2. Julie Meyer, *Dreams and Supernatural Encounters* (Shippensburg, PA: Destiny Image Publishers) 317.

Chapter Seventeen

THE END?

IN A FEW MINUTES, YOU WILL COMPLETE THIS BOOK, CLOSE THE cover, and place it on your shelf (or leave it in your e-library, as the case may be). My hope in writing this book was to leave you feeling confident and equipped in stepping into and growing in the gift of prophecy. My desire beyond that was to inspire and make you thirst for a deeper revelation of the heart of God and to make the connection between His heart and the flow of prophecy. I trust in reading these pages you have been challenged and encouraged to begin to step out in this gift of prophecy and to find new ways for your gift to increase. But is there more?

I remember the first time someone asked me the questions, "Where do you want to be with God in a year? In three years? In five years?" I was taken aback a little by the questions. The idea of charting a course toward spiritual maturity and increased gifting with specific goals and defined expectations was new to me at the time. First, I found the concept exciting. I even daydreamed about how I would spend time with God and what kind of supernatural activity and gifts I could see in my life. My excitement was toned down a little when I started to put a plan together, beginning with the vision I wanted to be heading toward. *This is going to take some work*, I thought. *Not a job for the faint of heart.*

In the years since, I have often fallen short of my goals, finding myself sidetracked with other things. At other times I have wondered "Am I really getting anywhere?" Then I realize I am farther than I would have been in my goal had I not kept moving forward, in spite of my weaknesses and inconsistencies. If I fail 50 percent of the time, I am still 50 percent farther along than if I hadn't done anything at all!

So I want to challenge you to think beyond conquering the gift of prophecy and moving on. Ask God for a vision of His heart for you and where He wants to take you in this gift. Catch a vision for a bigger picture and find your place in the story line. He has great things in store for you. As Hebrews 12:1 admonishes us, set your course and stay in the race.

Some days our impact will seem minimal; other days we will rejoice in our hearts for the people we have touched with our prophetic words. I want to emphasize again that *you* count, you are valuable to God, and what you do makes a difference. Your face is beautiful to Him, and your voice is sweet! Connect your heart to His heart and prophesy! Set a course and get some vision for where you want to be with your gift in a year or five years! Ask the Lord for a spirit of wisdom and understanding to see the best ways to love Him and to love your neighbor through this precious gift. Think in terms of how you can serve the body by prophesying. Make some clear plans of how you can get there and persevere, stay faithful. When you fall down, get back up and keep going.

In the process, make time and find ways to go deep in God's heart. Learn to let Abba lavish His affections on you and allow Jesus, as your Bridegroom King, to kiss you with the kisses of His Word. Fill yourself with His Word and learn to encounter Him through praying Scripture. The deeper your heart, the stronger your words will be.

I pray the Lord's blessing be with you as you set a course for a lifelong journey with God. May you increase in your prophetic gifting and impact those whose paths you cross, encouraging them to stay in the race and to find their place in the divine story line. Is this the end of the story? I don't think so. *The Beginning* sounds more like it!

ABOUT JEFF EGGERS

JEFF EGGERS WAS RADICALLY SAVED DURING THE JESUS MOVE-ment in 1970 and has over 40 years of ministry experience, including several years of pastoral ministry and leadership. From 2004 through 2014 he served as an "intercessory missionary" at the International House of Prayer in Kansas City, Missouri. In that capacity he also served on the prophetic leadership team, where he gave leadership to the prophecy and healing teams as well as taught and equipped in various internships and the IHOP Bible School. Intimacy and prayer, growing in the prophetic, healing and deliverance, and the ministry of the Holy Spirit are a few of the topics he taught regularly. He has also traveled widely, doing conferences and seminars in the states and abroad. Jeff is currently serving on the staff of the Blessed International Revival Center in Anaheim, California, where he oversees the House of Prayer-Orange County and continues to train and equip the saints. If you would be interested in having Jeff speak to your church or group, you may contact him at awordfromthewall@gmail.com.